]

MODERN PERSI

MW01284554

ENGAGING TORAH:
Modern Perspectives on the Hebrew Bible

Edited by
Walter Homolka
and
Aaron Panken

HEBREW UNION COLLEGE PRESS

HEBREW UNION COLLEGE PRESS
© 2018 Hebrew Union College Press

Set in ITC Legacy Serif by Raphaël Freeman, Renana Typesetting

Printed in the United States of America

Library of Congress Cataloging-in-Publication Data

Names: Homolka, Walter, editor. | Panken, Aaron D., editor.
Title: Engaging Torah : modern perspectives on the Hebrew Bible / edited by
  Walter Homolka and Aaron Panken.
Other titles: Modern perspectives on the Hebrew Bible
Description: Cincinnati, Ohio : Hebrew Union College Press, 2018
Identifiers: LCCN 2017058894 | ISBN 978-0-87820-159-4
Subjects: LCSH: Bible. Old Testament--Criticism, interpretation, etc.
Classification: LCC BS1178.H4 E54 2018 | DDC 221.6/1--dc23
LC record available at https://lccn.loc.gov/2017058894

This book is dedicated to Rüdiger Liwak,
in gratitude for his immense achievement as
Executive Editor of the Philippson Tanakh
(2013–2018)

Contents

Acknowledgments

THE EDITORS WOULD LIKE TO THANK DAVID AARON, CO-CHAIR of the Board of Directors of HUC Press, for the initiative and inspiration that made this book happen, as well as Rüdiger Liwak and Hanna Liss, the co-editors of the German Philippson *Tanakh* which is the basis for this English volume. We would also like to thank Sonja Rethy, Editorial Director of HUC Press, for handling the book in a most ingenious and competent way, as well as Alisa Rethy for her translations from the German. Finally, we are grateful to Oxford University Press for providing us with the permission to publish Bernard Levenson's text, and to The Leo Baeck Foundation, whose support helped make this book possible. HUC Press and Abraham Geiger College at the University of Potsdam would also like to acknowledge the unique efforts of Herder Publishers Freiburg for revising one of the great German translations of the Hebrew Bible for today. The three volumes of the Ludwig Philippson *Tanakh* were published between 2015 and 2018.

Walter Homolka
Aaron Panken

February, 2018

Preface

AARON PANKEN

Hebrew Union College – Jewish Institute of Religion

THE BIBLE IS UNDOUBTEDLY THE STARTING POINT OF JUDAISM.
Within its pages are the laws, ideals, narratives, and poetry that
shape every generation of Jewish thought, initiating vast trajecto-
ries of interpretation, jurisprudence, argumentation, and literary
and artistic creation – a process which began millennia ago yet
continues fervently today. Wherever Jews lived, whatever language
they spoke, the Bible remained a core text read publicly and regularly, studied and taught incessantly, shaping a common cultural
language that spanned generations and geography. Love for the
Bible and the creative interpretive possibilities it brought into being
carried Jews through times both agreeable and awful, uniting them
as a single people in service to their God.

Ask any Jewish individual which text is the faith's most sacred,
and the universal answer will be: the Torah, comprising Genesis,
Exodus, Leviticus, Numbers, and Deuteronomy. The name "Torah"
arises from the Hebrew root *y-r-h*, meaning "to teach." Its name,
therefore, means "teaching" or "learning." The word *torah* appears
within the Torah itself (including in Lev 6:7, 7:1, 7:37–38 and 14:54–56;
Num 6:21; Deut 4:44 and 33:4), where it means a collection of laws
or rules. The term *Torat Moshe* (the Torah of Moses) is used in the
Prophets and may refer to the Five Books of Moses (see Josh 1:7;
Ezra 3:2 and 7:6; Mal 3:22), suggesting that some version could have
been extant and was already considered holy by the time these
works were written.

Explanations of the Torah's origin vary significantly across the streams of Jewish life: some view it as divinely revealed in its entirety at Mount Sinai; others see it as the result of centuries of editing by various authors with their own political, religious, and moral agendas drawing heavily upon texts and customs of the surrounding Ancient Near East; others, still, find a middle point in which individual divine revelations led to acts of inspired writing and editing within particular cultural environments. However one happens to view the Torah's derivation, it occupies a uniquely revered place in the Jewish canon, and serves as the key source in the development of later Jewish literatures, from the Dead Sea Scrolls, Greco-Roman Jewish writings, and rabbinic literature, to later Jewish prayer books, medieval commentary and poetry, and more recent post-Enlightenment works that grapple with its place in a very different contemporary world. What is certain is that the entirety of the Jewish people, despite their significant differences in outlook, agree that the Torah, predominantly, and the Bible to a slightly lesser extent, are sacred and form the basis for the development of the life of the Jewish people.

During the past three centuries scholars have radically reinterpreted both the Jewish and the Christian relationship with Scripture. While prior Jewish commentators like Ibn Ezra would highlight challenges within the biblical text (contradictions, anachronisms and the like), such discrepancies were often viewed as exceptional, and were generally dismissed as valid evidence for disproving the unity of the Torah itself. The seventeenth-century philosopher Baruch Spinoza was among the first to question publicly Moses's authorship of the Torah, which eventually led to his expulsion from the Jewish community. Undeterred, he outlined new ways of reading the entire Bible that defined new pathways of interpretation extended by scholars ever since. There now exist more nuanced and variegated ways of reading that bring together the disparate fields of archaeology, history, source criticism, comparative Ancient Near Eastern studies, literary criticism, feminist and queer readings, alongside many other approaches, to render the Bible meaningful in the contemporary world. While the concept of the Bible as objectively true in any historical sense has diminished, the possibilities for creating meaningful and relevant readings in an age dominated by science has been renewed and broadened in inspiring ways.

The volume at hand is one that follows a long and honorable tradition of familiarizing present-day readers with the Bible and its scholarly context in a variety of different languages. It is an extension of a recent revision and republication of an older German work completed in 1854, *Die Tora: Die Fünf Bücher Mose und die Prophetenlesungen (hebräisch-deutsch) in der Übersetzung von Rabbiner Ludwig Philippson* (The Torah: The Five Books of Moses and the Prophetic Readings (in Hebrew and German) in the translation of Rabbi Ludwig Philippson).[1] Philippson (1811–1889) was a prominent member of the *haskalah* movement, which aimed to increase the knowledge of Jews across Europe and help them overcome ignorance and superstition. His writing provided a German translation and commentary, as well as scholarly introductions to each of the books of the Torah and a general introduction to the Prophets.

This volume brings a similar work to the English-speaking world. Its goal is to offer succinct, readable, yet high-level introductions to each of the books of the Torah, as well as general information on the Prophets and Writings. It is intended for readers who are looking to learn more of the scholarly background that allows these texts to be read from an informed and contemporary perspective. It does not include the texts themselves, as there are numerous versions available for English speakers that can provide text and line-by-line commentary. It is written by respected scholars from around the world, including professors from the Abraham Geiger College at the University of Potsdam, Hebrew Union College - Jewish Institute of Religion in the United States and Israel, the Ziegler School of Rabbinic Studies of American Jewish University in Los Angeles,

---

1 The essays in this volume on the Five Books of Moses and the Haftarot, as well as "The Torah in Jewish Life from the Nineteenth Century until Today," appeared in the 2015 German *Die Tora* (Herder). The general Introduction and Preface, as well as the introductions to *Nevi'im* and *Ketuvim* are new to this American edition.

Leo Baeck College in London, the Jewish Theological Seminary in New York, as well as other fine institutions. It represents a global effort to provide vital background to the study of the Bible in an accessible way that incorporates the learning of over nearly two centuries of modern Jewish scholarship.

If you are a student of the Bible, we hope this work will broaden your horizons, helping you to bring new scholarly ideas into your understanding of ancient texts, and to go beyond, as Philippson might have characterized it, ignorance and superstition. In this respect, it continues the awesome project of creating and interpreting sacred texts begun so many centuries ago under vastly different circumstances. Our part in such a project, when done best, is to enable each and every contemporary Jew (and, of course, others) to find their own meaning in these sacred texts, to realize the extraordinary learning that can result from interacting with them, and to do so in a mode that respects and builds upon all the lessons that modern humanities and science can bring to that interaction. Only through such complete approaches to the text can meaning and truth, in their deepest sense, arise.

An Introduction to *Engaging Torah*

WALTER HOMOLKA

Abraham Geiger College at the University of Potsdam

THIS BOOK AIMS TO ELUCIDATE THE HEBREW BIBLE'S ROLE AS
the cornerstone of faith for "the people of the book." In doing so
it will examine its structure, the subject matter of its individual
books, and the ways in which it can be interpreted.

The Hebrew Bible – which differs from its Christian counter-
parts in its content and in the order of its books – is divided into
three main sections: Torah ("Instruction"), *Nevi'im* ("Prophets"),
and *Ketuvim* ("Writings," also referred to as "Hagiography"). The
acronym *"Tanakh"* is derived from these sections' initial letters.

Within the Five Books of Moses, the word "Torah" can be translated as "instruction" or as "law." These two meanings illustrate the
dual role the Torah plays within Jewish life. Recited aloud at the
synagogue, or read privately in the home, the Torah is primarily a
book of instruction, albeit often couched in history and narrative;
through its 613 commandments and prohibitions, however, it is
also a book of law. The division of the Bible into weekly portions
reflects their role in the synagogue's reading service, and each book's
name also functions as the title of the Shabbat on which it is read.
This is how the first book of Moses, for example, gets its Hebrew
name, *Bereishit*, "In the Beginning," which is also the name of the
first Shabbat in the reading cycle.

Translated from the German by Alisa Rethy.

THE TORAH READING

Every new Torah scroll must be copied by hand onto parchment, in impeccable calligraphy, without any personal embellishments. The strict guidelines for this work were likely established by the Masoretes of the eighth century. Within the synagogue, the scrolls are kept in handcrafted cloth mantles, or in chests which are sumptuously decorated and often adorned with silver jewelry.

During the synagogue service, people who are considered "of age" according to religious law are called to the Ark in order to commence and conclude each section of the Torah reading through particular benedictions. In addition to these blessings, such an individual is also among those responsible for monitoring the quality of the reading, stopping the reader if he or she makes a mistake. During weekday services three people are called to the Torah; at the beginning of the month (new moon) four; on holidays five; on Yom Kippur six, and on Shabbat seven. It is considered a great honor to read the Torah blessings, and, for this reason, on the High Holidays sometimes congregation members would donate large sums of money to charity in exchange for the privilege. Today, however, it is generally frowned upon to "purchase" the call to the Torah, which in Hebrew is called an "*aliyah*" – an "ascent" or "summons."

The Torah is divided into fifty-four portions (parashiyot), each of which is read over the course of the Jewish year. The Babylonian Talmud indicates that at that time in the land of Israel (ca. 200–500 CE) a three-year reading cycle was standard, with one-third of each week's portion recited each Shabbat. This three-year cycle was supplanted by a reading of the entire parashah over the course of the centuries, but was reintroduced in the middle of the nineteenth century as part of the Jewish Reform movement and is now typical in Reform and many Conservative congregations. In addition to the reading from the Books of Moses, on each Shabbat a shorter portion from selected books of the Prophets is also read. While evidence for readings from the Prophets dates to the first century BCE, the actual assignment of specific passages likely became commonplace only centuries later. The haftarah is always connected through its subject matter to its respective parashah, although the connection is not always immediately evident. Generally, an eighth person is summoned to carry out this reading.

The text is read according to a system of cantillation – a system of pitches. Tonal marks, or *ta'amim*, guide the chanting of the Torah and highlight the structure and meaning of the text. These marks, however, are not included in the handwritten Torah scrolls; they only appear in printed books which are used to prepare for the reading or which are used by congregants as they follow along. The reading of the text functions as its first interpretation, so it is of great importance that a real expert, a "master of the reading" (*ba'al qorei*), carries out the recitation. In contrast, the haftarah can, as a rule, be recited by any member of the congregation and is read from printed books which include the tonal marks. During the reading, the congregation follows along in these printed books which, in addition to the tonal marks, generally also contain commentary and translations.

The Jewish holidays also have a fixed program of readings from the Five Books of Moses and the Prophets. Each holiday is assigned a particular selection of passages, which are located at various points within the scroll. If a single scroll were to be used for these readings, it would need to be rolled after the first reading to the starting point of the second passage – a process which, unlike with a bound book, is quite time-consuming. Therefore, on such occasions more than one Torah scroll is "lifted" from the Ark.

Occasionally Shabbat will coincide with a holiday, which further increases the number of Torah scrolls in use. In the ceremony of taking out and returning the Torah to the Ark, the scroll is carried through the synagogue by a member of the congregation. During this procession, everyone in the congregation touches the scroll with the tassels of their prayer shawls or with a prayer book, which they then kiss. When a person returns to their seat after chanting the blessings before the reading of the text, it is customary to shake this person's hand in recognition. This not only acknowledges the reader, but is also meant to bring congregants into closer contact with the Torah, since, when the blessing is recited, a person comes into direct contact with the scroll, holding it by its two wooden handles. In addition, before reciting the blessing, one who has been called to the Torah wraps the tassels of his or her prayer shawl around their finger (or uses a prayer book) and touches the point in the text where the reading commences and ends. In Reform, Conservative, and Reconstructionist synagogues, women and men participate equally in all of these activities.

The Torah scroll thus acquires a nearly sacred significance, although, in the Reform movement, this type of veneration is sometimes rejected as coming too close to idolatry. On the High Holidays the Ark is opened during the most important prayers, in order to give the prayers more significance through the "aura" that radiates from the scrolls, and, because the scrolls are housed at the eastern wall of the synagogue, this also reflects an attempt to ascend higher on the scale of holiness by turning toward Jerusalem. Funding the writing or acquisition of a Torah scroll is highly regarded – a single scroll requires about a year to complete, and can cost approximately $20,000 dollars or more. The mantles which cover the scrolls are also often donated.

THE WEEKLY READING FROM THE TORAH AND THE HAFTAROT

Shabbat	Torah Portion	Haftarah
Bereishit	Gen 1:1–6:8	Isaiah 42:5–43:10
Noah	Gen 6:9–11:32	Isaiah 54:1–55:5
Lekh Lekha	Gen 12:1–17:27	Isaiah 40:27–41:16
Va-yera	Gen 18:1–22:24	2 Kings 4:1–37
Hayyei Sarah	Gen 23:1–25:18	1 Kings 1:1–31
Toledot	Gen 25:19–28:9	Malakhi 1:1–2:7
Va-yeitzei	Gen 28:10–32:3	Hosea 12:13–14
Va-yishlah	Gen 32:4–36:43	Hosea 11:7–12:12

Shabbat	Torah Portion	Haftarah
Va-yeishev	Gen 37:1–40:23	Amos 2:6–3:8
Miqqetz	Gen 41:1–44:17	1 Kings 3:15–4:1
Va-yiggash	Gen 44:18–47:27	Ezekiel 37:15–28
Va-yehi	Gen 47:28–50:26	1 Kings 2:1–12
Shemot	Ex 1:1–6:1	Isaiah 27:6–28:13
Va-eira	Ex 6:2–9:35	Isaiah 43:1–12
Bo	Ex 10:1–13:16	Jeremiah 46:13–28
Be-shallah	Ex 13:17–17:16	Judges 4:4–5:31
Yitro	Ex 18:1–20:23	Isaiah 6:1–7:6
Mishpatim	Ex 21:1–24:18	Jeremiah 34:8–22; 33:25–26
Terumah	Ex 25:1–27:19	1 Kings 5:26–6:13
Tetzaveh	Ex 27:20–30:10	Ezekiel 43:10–27
Ki Tissa	Ex 30:11–34:35	1 Kings 18:1–39
Va-yaqheil	Ex 35:1–38:20	1 Kings 7:40–50
Pequdei	Ex 38:21–40:38	1 Kings 7:51–8:21
Va-yiqra	Lev 1:1–5:26	Isaiah 43:21–44:23
Tzav	Lev 6:1–8:36	Jeremiah 7:21–8:3; 9:22–23
Shemini	Lev 9:1–11:47	2 Samuel 6:1–7:17
Tazria	Lev 12:1–13:59	2 Kings 5:1–19
Metzora	Lev 14:1–15:33	2 Kings 7:3–20
Aharei Mot	Lev 16:1–18:30	Ezekiel 22:1–16
Kedoshim	Lev 19:1–20:27	Amos 9:7–15
Emor	Lev 21:1–24:23	Ezekiel 44:15–31

Shabbat	Torah Portion	Haftarah
Be-har	Lev 25:1–26:2	Jeremiah 32:6–27
Be-ḥuqqotai	Lev 26:3–27:34	Jeremiah 16:19–17:14
Be-midbar	Num 1:1–4:20	Hosea 2:1–22
Naso	Num 4:21–7:89	Judges 13:2–25
Be-ha'alotkha	Num 8:1–12:16	Zechariah 2:14–4,7
Shelaḥ Lekha	Num 13:1–15:41	Joshua 2:1–24
Qoraḥ	Num 16:1–18:32	1 Samuel 11:14–12:22
Ḥuqqat	Num 19:1–22:1	Judges 11:1–33
Balaq	Num 22:2–25:9	Micah 5:6–6:8
Pinḥas	Num 25:10–30:1	1 Kings 18:46–19:21
Mattot	Num 30:2–32:42	Jeremiah 1:1–2:3
Masei	Num 33:1–36:13	Jeremiah 2:4–28; 3:4
Devarim	Deut 1:1–3:22	Isaiah 1:1–27
Va-etḥannan	Deut 3:23–7:11	Isaiah 40:1–26
Eiqev	Deut 7:12–11:25	Isaiah 49:14–51:3
Re'eh	Deut 11:26–16:17	Isaiah 54:11–55:5
Shoftim	Deut 16:18–21:9	Isaiah 51:12–52:12
Ki Teitzei	Deut 21:10–25:19	Isaiah 54:1–10
Ki Tavo	Deut 26:1–29:8	Isaiah 60:1–22
Nitzavim	Deut 29:9–30:20	Isaiah 61:10–63:9
Va-yeilekh	Deut 31:1–30	Isaiah 55:6–13; 56:1–8
Ha'azinu	Deut 32:1–52	2 Samuel 22:1–51
Ve-zot Ha-berakhah	Deut 33:1–34:12	Joshua 1:1–18

In this overview, the weekly Torah portions and haftarot are presented according to the Ashkenazic tradition. In the Sephardic tradition and in Jewish Reform congregations some differences exist with respect to the selections from the Prophets. Also, some synagogues, as noted, operate on a triennial reading cycle.

TORAH INTERPRETATION: "THE FOURFOLD MEANING"

The oldest cohesive interpretation of the Torah is probably Targum Onkelos. His translation into Aramaic, written in the second century CE, is still printed today in all Rabbinic Bibles.[1]

The guiding assumption of traditional Bible interpretation is that no errors are to be found among all 304,805 letters of the Torah; the work of interpretation resolves any and all contradictions, repetitions, divergences, and apparent grammatical errors. The basic model for the traditional technique of interpretation is the so-called PaRDeS:

- Pa for "*peshat*," the explicit meaning
- R for "*remmez*," an interpretation through linguistic hints and/or numerical symbolism
- De for "*derash*," the interpretative meaning (from the same root as *midrash*)
- S for "*sod*," the esoteric or mystical meaning

Within the nearly innumerable exegeses on the Hebrew Bible that have developed over the millennia, the most influential commentary is likely that of the eleventh-century Rabbi Shlomo Ben Yitzchak, better known as Rashi, who wrote commentary to the entire Bible. In his commentary, Rashi attempted to resolve apparent contradictions between individual passages. He championed the literal meaning (*peshat*), avoided "hints" and number clues (*remmez*), only occasionally mentions narrative interpretations (*derash*), and very seldom mentions the mystical interpretation (*sod*).

---

1 The Rabbinic Bible was first published in Vienna in 1524. Rabbinic Bibles, in addition to Targum Onkelos, include the Hebrew and Aramaic text of the *Tanakh*, Masoretic notes on the biblical text, Aramaic Targums, and Rashi's commentary.

His commentary is still printed today in all conventional annotated versions of the Bible, and is considered to be the standard work of Jewish exegesis.

Rashi interprets, for example, the (in)famous passage "an eye for an eye" (Exod 21:24) as follows: If a person has destroyed the eye of another, he should compensate him with the value of his eye. This worth is calculated on the market, by considering to what extent a one-eyed slave is assigned lesser value than one with both eyes. All similar cases should be handled in this manner, without literally removing the limb of the offender.

For the twenty-first century, two particularly influential commentaries on the Five Books of Moses and the haftarot deserve mention: first, the commentary compiled by the Chief Rabbi of Great Britain, Joseph Herman Hertz (1872–1946), and second, the commentary of Rabbi W. Gunther Plaut (1912–2012), which is available in English, German, Russian, and Portuguese. Because these works engage widely with the scholarly biblical criticism of the nineteenth and twentieth centuries and are, through their use of vernacular languages, accessible for those who have little knowledge of Hebrew, they have made their way into thousands of Jewish households. Hertz notes in his preface: "Take whatever is beautiful, regardless of its source, even if it is from the works of a pious Christian commentator or a radical Jewish or non-Jewish scholar."

At the end of the reading the Torah is held up by a member of the congregation (the Hebrew term for this ritual is *hagba'a*) and the congregation exclaims "This is the Torah that Moses set before the Israelites by the command of the Lord...." Jewish biblical interpretations point out that, although the plural pronoun would be the natural choice in the context of the nation awaiting the revelation of the Torah, the singular is used: the text says "*it* stood," not "they stood." While scholarly biblical criticism considers this to be a scribal error, traditional interpretation sees the use of the singular as conveying an added layer of meaning, illustrating that the nation was fully unified in spirit and received the Torah as a single being. This interpretation underscores the unsurpassable significance of the Torah in Jewish life. It is is a book of the people in every sense of the term, and, even at the beginning of the twenty-first century, is surely the most-read and most-cited work of the entire Jewish tradition. The Hebrew Bible, its reading and interpretation, is the backbone of Jewish life. As Heinrich Heine (1797–1856) fittingly described it, the Torah is the "portable homeland" of the Jews.

The Torah in Jewish Life from the Nineteenth Century until Today

TAMARA COHN ESKENAZI

Hebrew Union College – Jewish Institute of Religion

IN THE SYNAGOGUE, WHEN THE TORAH IS RETURNED TO THE holy ark, it is customary to chant in Hebrew the following words from the Book of Proverbs: "*Etz ḥayyim hi,....*" "It is a tree of life for all who take hold of it, and those who hold it fast will be blessed" (Prov 3:18).

As this liturgical recitation shows, Jews recognize the Torah as a tree of life that, unlike the remote primordial tree in the Garden of Eden, is now planted in the midst of the community. As a "tree of life" the Torah has the power to sustain and renew those who live uprightly in the presence of God.

For thousands of years Jewish communities took steps to ensure that the people would have access to this vital source, and that it would remain the prized possession of all Jews. The weekly public readings of the Torah secured its presence in the midst of the community, not only as an object to revere, but as a teaching to practice in all aspects of life. The translation of the Torah into the languages of diverse Jewish communities – following a tradition that began (according to the Talmud) with Ezra in the fifth century BCE – ensured that these teachings would reach all Jews: women, men, and children, not merely the educated or affluent elite.

Nehemiah 8–10 depicts the occasion at which the Torah was placed at the center of Jewish communal life and became a source for Jewish practice. In that public ceremony, when all the people gathered – men and women together – Ezra the priest and scribe stood on a special platform above the crowd. As he opened the scroll of the Torah, the people rose up in reverence. When Ezra offered a blessing, all bowed down and proclaimed, "Amen, Amen" (Neh 8:1–6). In due course, after hearing the Torah's messages, the people implemented its teachings. In the millennia that followed, Jews continued to find ways to study Torah and apply its teachings to all areas of life, both in public and at home, developing a complex network of practices and values. Because it fostered a commitment to the covenant and to God, and led to all other virtues deemed vital for Jewish thriving, Torah study came to be regarded as a sacred obligation.

The role of the Torah and the practices it generated, as well as the larger meanings that these convey, were all challenged by modernity. By the nineteenth century, following the Western Enlightenment and the gradual granting of legal rights to Jews – the Emancipation – Jews confronted new and difficult questions. The Torah, a homeland for millennia, became a turf upon which battles were fought in order to define and reframe what it meant to be a Jew in the modern world. Perceived tension between "reason," so valued by the Enlightenment, and "revelation," so essential in the Torah, undermined rabbinic authority which for centuries had created the rules and interpretations through which the Torah was translated into life. Not only was rabbinic authority challenged, but the Torah itself came under fire. New scholarly approaches (that began with Spinoza in the seventeenth century, but gained wide-ranging popularity in the nineteenth), claimed that the Torah was neither by God nor by Moses; it was argued, instead, that the Torah was a composite of distinct documents written by several authors, all of them considerably later than Moses.

Jews responded in a variety of ways. In Western Europe, this challenge initially led to a bifurcation, pitting those who claimed to be progressive or liberal against those who claimed to be traditional or orthodox.

Rabbi Abraham Geiger, in the nineteenth century, was an early proponent of progressive or Reform Judaism, a movement that regarded the rabbinic traditions of the Talmud and their ramifications as no longer applicable to the modern world. Recognized as one of the fathers of Reform Judaism, Geiger acknowledged the validity of new theories about the development of the Torah, but nonetheless upheld the Torah as a decisive source for Jews. According to Geiger, "The Bible is now and has always been an ever-living Word, not a dead letter. It has spoken to all generations and imparted its teachings to them.... This is the reason why every age, every movement, and every personality in history has brought its own ideas to bear upon the Bible, hence the multitude of elaborations, interpretations, and typical and symbolic attempts at explanation."[1]

Geiger sought to establish this new branch of Judaism on the scientific study of history, without assuming that any Jewish text was divinely written. Opposing him was Rabbi Samson Raphael Hirsch, regarded as the father of modern Orthodoxy. According to Hirsch, the Torah could only be understood properly through a rabbinic lens. In his comment to Exodus 21:2 he likened the written Torah to "short notes on a full and extensive lecture by any scholarly master."[2] Although these notes suffice to enable students who were present at the lecture to recall the entire lecture, they are all but useless for those who did *not* hear the master's lecture. For Hirsch, the rabbinic tradition is where the fuller lecture is discovered.[3]

These debates were followed by a further splitting of Judaism, eventually into four major movements: Reform/Liberal (or Progressive), Orthodox (including Modern Orthodox, Ultra-Orthodox and Haredi, along with other groupings), Conservative, and Reconstructionist, each establishing institutions for ordaining rabbis, and each offering distinct ways to continue to apply the Torah to

---

1 Quoted by Alan T. Levenson in his *The Making of the Modern Jewish Bible: How Scholars in Germay, Israel, and America Transformed an Ancient Text* (Lanham, MD: Rowman and Littlefield, 2011), p. 47.

2 Levenson, p. 50.

3 Hirsch's commentary, 1867-78. English Edition: *Terumat Tzvi: The Pentateuch with a Translation by Samson Raphael Hirsch*, ed. Ephraim Oratz (New York: Judaica Press, 1986).

changed circumstances. The Enlightenment also generated a new phenomenon: the secular or cultural Jew who does not consider the age-old Jewish teachings and practices relevant, or even knows them.

In the early years of the twentieth century, Franz Rosenzweig bemoaned the results of the Jewish encounter with modernity in Western Europe. In "On Being a Jewish Person," Rosenzweig diagnosed the impact of outside forces on Judaism. He claimed that the old Jewish law, the Jewish home, and the synagogue service that sustained Jewish life exist still, "but because they are now only parts of this life, they are no longer what they were when they were joined together."[4]

Rosenzweig concluded that "It is to a book, the Book, that we owe our survival…The learning of this book became an affair of the people, filling the bounds of Jewish life, completely. Everything was really within this learning of the Book.…"[5] Now, however, a new learning was necessary, because Jews had wandered off from that Jewish center, and were unable to find their way back. This new learning needed to be "A learning that no longer starts from the Torah and leads into life, but the other way around, from life, from a world that knows nothing of the Law or pretends to know nothing, back to the Torah. That is the sign of our time."[6]

The Shoah/Holocaust made internal Jewish tensions irrelevant, but raised the challenge to Jewish trust in the meaning and value of the Torah to a new height. Some saw the failure of divine and human intervention as a sign that the teachings of the Torah do not apply to our time. For others, the Torah was a sustaining source, at times precisely because of the absence of other manifestations of necessary hope.

The Yanov Torah (now at HUC-JIR, Los Angeles) is an example. This scroll was reassembled from portions of buried Torah scrolls

---

4   From Rosenzweig, "Bildung und kein Ende," in *Kleinere Schriften*, pp. 79–93. Cited in N.N. Glazer, *Franz Rosenzweig: His Life and Thought* (New York: Schocken Books, 1976), 218–19.

5   Ibid., 228.

6   Glatzer, 231; from *Kleinere Schriften*, pp. 94–99.

that inmates smuggled into the concentration camp at Yanov. The risk these people took demonstrates the extraordinary power of the Torah to generate courage, resourcefulness, and hope even in the midst of unspeakable horror. This story also symbolizes how Jewish ways of life were reassembled in the aftermath of the Shoah/Holocaust.

Throughout the modern era the different Jewish movements emphasized the diverse ways in which the Torah applies to life. Orthodox Jews insist on the Mosaic or Sinaitic origin of both the written Torah and the concomitant oral traditions postulated by classical halakhic, i.e., rabbinic, legal process. Conservative Jews regard the written Torah as the foundational text of Judaism and "the teaching par excellence about God's relationship to the world and to the Jewish people."[7] Although Conservative Jews recognize rabbinic halakhah as binding, they view halakhah's development in historical terms and are more liberal in their legal interpretations than Orthodox deciders. Reform or liberal Jews view the Torah as divinely inspired, but written by human hands and in the language of the time in which it was created. Although the notion of an obligatory halakhah is contested, there are practitioners of Reform halakhah. Reconstructionist Jews view the Torah as the Jewish people's response to God's presence in the world.

Challenges to the authority of the Torah notwithstanding, the public reading of the Torah, modeled on Nehemiah 8, continued in the modern era as the cornerstone of Jewish worship in the synagogue on Shabbat as well as on Mondays and Thursdays (ancient times' market days, used as an opportunity to make the Torah accessible to all). The ancient rabbinic division of the Torah into weekly portions, and readings for special occasions, continues to provide the world-wide-web through which Jews experience a shared journey. All movements in Judaism largely follow the same sequence. Consequently, regardless of where in the world Jews might find themselves at any particular time, they can expect to discover the same Torah portion (parashah) read in the synagogue.

---

7 *Etz Hayim*, ed. David L. Lieber (New York: Jewish Publication Society, 2001), xvii.

Public reading of the Torah was for centuries the prerogative of men, with the Bar Mitzvah ("son of commandment") at age thirteen indicating that a boy has become qualified as legitimate member of the community. At this time, the youngster is called up to read from the Torah (referred to as an *aliyah*, "going up").

Two aspects of this practice were challenged in the modern era. Some argued that a thirteen-year-old boy is too young to be regarded as a Jewish adult. They proposed postponing the event to a later age and suggested a rite of "Confirmation" instead. Despite the appeal of this change, the Bar Mitzvah at age thirteen remains the norm, although some communities add Confirmation at a later point. The other challenge pertains to issues of gender. In 1922 the influential Jewish thinker and founder of Reconstructionism, Mordecai M. Kaplan, held the first public celebration of a girl's – his daughter's – Bat Mitzvah, and the ceremony spread widely among all liberal movements. The range of participation of women in regular synagogue services, however, evolved only gradually, and at a different pace for each movement. Regina Jonas of Berlin eloquently championed equal roles for women, including ordination as rabbis, basing her conclusions on the Talmud and other authoritative sources. She was privately ordained in 1935, but was shortly after killed in Auschwitz. Women in the modern era undertook important roles in Jewish religious life, and were already encouraged to have equal roles by Reform leaders like Isaac M. Wise in the late nineteenth century. But it was only in the aftermath of the ordination of women as rabbis, beginning with HUC-JIR's ordination of Sally Priesand in 1972, that women in the liberal movements regularly assumed full participation, including in the public reading of the Torah (*leinen*). While the circle of Orthodox women who are trained to do read Torah is expanding daily, the extent to which they can publically employ their skills varies in different Orthodox communities.

All Jewish movements attempt to define a relation to the Torah and to traditional Jewish practices and laws in order to preserve a living continuity with the past and to renew its contributions. All seek to follow the earlier practice of endowing everyday life with sanctity, but they achieve their goals in different ways and often by means of different rationales. For example: although kashrut was regarded by Reform Jews initially as irrelevant, currently all four movements engage food laws at some level, recognizing them as a distinct Jewish way to implement God's teachings in the most basic aspects of life. Certain Jews valorize humanistic ethics as a relevant feature of the laws, in addition to or in lieu of commandedness. Some redefine what counts as kosher or "fit to eat" by using ecological criteria, or regard forms of dietary laws as a means to fuller identification with the Jewish people. Issues such as whether farmhands receive living wages, or whether chickens are cage-free, have been part of new discussions of what is "fit to eat," i.e., kosher, in certain circles. Blessings and other rituals continue to hallow meals and other daily and unique events, but new language for how God is addressed or perceived has also come into use. For example, the Shekhinah, a mystical term for the divine immanence imaged as feminine, may be invoked as the source of blessing. For some, the attempt to be Jewishly hospitable has prompted adopting those laws that would allow a wide spectrum of Jewish inclusivity, yet do not exclude non-Jews.

Torah study has regained its prominent place in Jewish life. New Torah commentaries have emerged in the USA, reflecting the range of identities that are coalescing around the Torah. These supplement or replace the English language Torah commentary that has been available since 1937, and has been widely used: *The Pentateuch and Haftorahs: Hebrew Text, English Translation and Commentary*, which was edited by J.H. Hertz. See, for example, the Reform Movement's *The Torah: A Modern Commentary* (Plaut), the Conservatives' *Etz Hayim*, the Orthodox's *The Stone Chumash*, and also commentaries such as *The Torah: A Women's Commentary* (Eskenazi and Weiss) and *The Modern Men's Torah Commentary* (Salkin) which include voices from the entire spectrum of Judaism. There are also commentaries by individuals such as Robert Alter, Everret Fox, and Richard Friedman, that emphasize the virtues of the Torah's significance as great literature, and reach out to secular as well as religious Jews.

This renaissance of commentaries, together with the resurgence

of Torah study throughout today's Jewish world (in homes, synagogues, schools, and even businesses) shows that even if modern
or postmodern readers do not find their way to God, they often
find their way back to the Jewish people via the Torah. Such devel-
opments illustrate how the Torah continues to root itself in these
homes, synagogues, and schools, as well as in the hearts, minds,
and deeds of the Jewish people.

Introduction to Genesis

ZIONY ZEVIT

American Jewish University

THE NAMES "GENESIS" AND "BEREISHIT"

The Book of Genesis is not a "book," as this word is usually understood, and "Genesis" does not refer to the creation of the cosmos from nothing as is usually understood.

"Genesis," used in many translations, derives from Greek, *génesis*, which refers to births, origins, or consequences. It was first used as the title for this composition by Jewish scholars who translated the Hebrew text into Greek in the third century BCE, as well as by the Jewish philosopher Philo of Alexandria in the first century CE. Jerome, who translated the book into Latin in the fourth century, kept the Greek title. European languages borrowed it from Jerome's Vulgate, used throughout Europe until the Reformation.

Genesis alludes to the Hebrew formula *'eilleh toledot*, "these are the origins/beginnings/births of 'x'," where "x" refers to people who have been previously mentioned and what happened to them. This phrase within the book bridges between consecutive narratives five times, and between narratives and genealogical lists five times as well. Translations usually render *"toledot"* according to context, variously as "story," "history," or "descendants," so English-language readers are often unaware that the same Hebrew formula is repeated ten times, as a recurring leitmotif (2:4; 6:9; 10:1; 11:10, 27; 25:12,19; 36:1,9; 37:2). The formula invariably informs readers that one event or set of circumstances gives rise to another, and that, consequently, there is a relationship between effects and prior causes, consequences and prior actions, actions and prior decisions. It implies that history is not simply one meaningless event after another, but rather that it is comprehensible, explicable, and meaningful.

Jews conventionally refer to the Book of Genesis by its first Hebrew word, "*Bereishit*" (1:1). This word is best translated literally in the context of the book's first verse as, "At the beginning/head of God's creating the heavens and the earth...." Bereishit, as the book's "title," is actually an abbreviation of the phrase *Ḥumash Bereishit*, "a fifth part, [called] Bereishit," while the complete Torah is called *Ḥamisha Ḥumshei Torah*, "the five fifths of Torah/Teaching." (The Greek equivalent of the phrase is Pentateuch, the whole that consists of five parts.) This way of referring to Genesis emphasizes that although it is a self-contained composition that may be studied independently from the remaining four-fifths of the Torah, it should simultaneously be viewed within the broader context of the whole Torah for which it provides an introduction.

The word Bereishit draws attention to the first chapter, which focuses on the zero point, teaching that quantifiable time and history began when God first formed a comprehensible cosmic order from pre-existing primordial stuff – dark matter, earth, water, and powerful wind. It informs readers that all humans are integrated into the organized cosmos, that God held all of his handiwork in high regard – "and God saw all that he had done and, behold, it was very good" (1:31) – and, finally, that units of time itself could be demarcated for special events and activities – made holy. Created things, material and immaterial, could be evaluated qualitatively, even time.

In his first comment on the Torah, Rashi, the most famous of the medieval commentators, explains why the Torah did not begin by listing the laws that God gave Israel at Sinai: the origin stories of Bereishit were presented first because the Torah authors wanted to provide the Jewish people with grounds for their right to the Promised Land. God, designer and master of the cosmos and the world known to humans, had designated a small part of his creation for his people and would allow them to settle it at a proper time in the future.

BEREISHIT AS RESPONSE

The narratives and genealogical lists in Bereishit indicate that our ancestors, the ancient Israelites, were interested in their origins. Bereishit consists of responses to questions asked by intelligent adults who lived in a small part of the ancient Near East 2600–3000 years ago: Where did we come from? Where did our ancient ancestors come from? Why are we in this place now and not in some other place? These questions demanded narrative answers that progressed from the far distant to the less distant past, and eventually concluded in the present of those posing them.

And, the responses to these questions, composed in what scholars call "Classical Biblical Hebrew," and following the literary conventions of the time when they were written, were meant to be interesting, relevant, and intelligible. It is clear, therefore, that both Bereishit and Genesis are appropriate names for the first part of the Pentateuch.

THE STRUCTURE AND CONTENTS OF BEREISHIT

After the story of the formation and organization of the cosmos that concludes with the manufacture of humans and of sacred time (1:26–27; 2:7), narratives in Bereishit focus on specific humans and their actions, but not only on humans. God, too, appears in some narratives, present in the world that he both created and declared to be "good." Where he appears, God is a pivotal actor, interacting – sometimes intimately and sometimes from a distance through dreams or messengers – with human characters. Bereishit informs its audience about God by describing what he did and sometimes explaining why, but not through abstract, doctrinal statements of the type that developed later, in the Hellenistic period.

The major characters in the narratives of Bereishit are God, Adam, Eve, humanity before the flood, Noah, humanity after the flood, Abraham, Sarah, Hagar, Ishmael, Isaac, Rebecca, Esau, Jacob, Rachel, Leah, and Joseph. Their stories are divided into fifty chapters, or twelve weekly Torah readings – parashiyot.

Chapter divisions in modern, printed Bibles were created by

Christian scholars during the medieval period and inserted into manuscripts for ease of reference. They were first introduced into Jewish Bible manuscripts used for study during the fourteenth century and later into Jewish printed Bibles for ease of reference so that Jews would be able to communicate with Christians about the Bible using a common system. (They are not allowed in the hand-written parchment scrolls used for public reading in the synagogue.) In contrast, the twelve weekly parashiyot are part of an elaborate division of the Torah into units of approximately equal length so that it can be read publicly and completed once a year. The system in use today follows a pattern invented by Jews in Babylon during the early medieval period.

Stories about the main characters of Bereishit fall into four major blocks:

(1) *The Primeval History* (Gen 1:1-11:32) presents a string of short, unconnected narratives – from the creation of the cosmos through the problematic early history of humanity – in two narrative cycles. The first covers ten generations from Adam to Noah, focusing on God's decision to wipe out almost all of Adam's descendants because they filled the earth with violence. He saves only Noah and his family because Noah was an ethical person. The second cycle covers the ten generations from Noah to Abraham, and tells the story of the Tower of Babel, explaining why humans, despite their common origin, speak many languages. Genealogies in this section clarifed for ancient Israelites that all peoples of the inhabited world known to them were descended from the three sons of Noah, and were, therefore, related to each other and to them.

This block of stories describes how God came to terms with the complicated nature of his human creatures: all were endowed with the ability to discern between good and bad, and between proper and improper behavior – a legacy from their ancestors in the Garden of Eden. They, therefore, could be held culpable for improper actions. God took it on himself to train them. In stories presented here, he did so by means of punishments, sometimes touched by mercy. After the flood, God reconciled himself to some shortcomings of his creatures and vowed never again to destroy all humanity by a cosmic flood. Thereafter, throughout the Bible, with the exception of the case of Sodom and Gomorrah, disasters involving catastrophic losses of human life are brought about by humans.

Not everything that people did at this early stage of human development was bad. They became agriculturalists and animal breeders, founded cities and invented crafts, developed viticulture, and organized nations. This socially complex, civilized world becomes the backdrop for the second block of stories.

The Primeval History closes by listing the descendants of Shem, son of Noah, and then focuses on the line of Terah, father of Abraham, mentioning that Sarah, Abraham's wife, was barren.

This block contains two of the twelve weekly readings (parashiyot), into which this book of the Torah is divided: Bereishit, and Noah. These divisions are universally cited by the first or second word of the parashah, transliterated and printed at the top of the page in versions of the Torah used for study as well as in Jewish translations.

(2) *The Abraham–Isaac Story Cycle* (12:1–25:26 and 26:1–34) begins with God's command that Abraham leave Mesopotamia and travel to a "land that He would show him," promising that he would become a great nation. Abraham sets out and arrives in the land of Canaan, where God promises him "this land." Later, God repeats his promise to a worried Abraham who has remained childless. Eventually, Abraham fathers two sons, Ishmael and Isaac, by different mothers. Isaac, the younger, born miraculously to the formerly childless Sarah after her menopause, is designated to produce the numerous descendents that would eventually inherit, that is, settle and control, Canaan. But even though God repeats the promise of land and progeny to Isaac when he is an adult, he fathers only twin sons by his wife Rebecca. The promise of progeny remains unfulfilled when the third narrative cycle begins at the end of chapter 25.

The stories in this section are divided over four weekly parashiyot: Lekh Lekha, Va-yera, Ḥayyei Sarah, and Toledot. Some narratives in Toledot, those that begin at 25:19 and end at 28:9, provide important background information and lead into the first part of the next collection of stories. (See 25:27–34 and 27:1–28:9.)

(3) *The Jacob Story Cycle* (25:27–34 and 27:1–36:43) concentrates initially on how Jacob, the younger of Isaac's two sons, tricks his brother Esau out of his rights as a first-born, and then tricks his blind father into blessing him with words intended for Esau. By virtue of his resourcefulness and talent for outfoxing people, Jacob achieves the position of heir to Abraham's promise. Whereas in the preceding story cycle God had designated that the younger son, Isaac, inherit his promise to Abraham, in this cycle, Jacob determines his own destiny.

To escape Esau's wrath, Jacob flees to the home of his duplicitous uncle Laban in Mesopotamia. Enroute, just before Jacob leaves the land of Canaan, God repeats the Abrahamic promise to him. Jacob wishes to marry Rachel, his uncle's younger daughter. Laban, however, tricks Jacob into marrying his older daughter Leah after Jacob has worked seven years for Rachel. But of his two wives, it is Leah who provides Jacob with most of his children; Rachel bears Joseph and dies during the birth of Benjamin. When Jacob returns to Canaan from Mesopotamia with married sons, and it seems possible that he will become "a nation," God again repeats the promise to him. The promise to Jacob will be repeated one more time, in the next group of narratives, when it appears that it will not be fulfilled.

Excluding the introductory narratives about Jacob and his family in Toledot, most of the stories in the Jacob Story Cycle are found in two parashiyot: Va-yeitzei and Va-yishlah.

(4) *The Joseph Story Cycle* (37:1–50:26), which continues the saga of Jacob's family, differs from the previous two sections of narrative. Whereas these presented short or independent narratives in sequence, narratives in this next cycle coalesce into a complicated story built from many scenes, some set in Canaan and some in Egypt, and peopled with many characters who are psychologically complex: Jacob, Joseph, Joseph's brothers, Potiphar's wife, and

Pharaoh. Story lines intersect, and characters in one narrative refer to events that happened in another.

The cycle narrates the story of Jacob's older sons, who, resentful of Jacob's special affection for Joseph and angry about Joseph's dreams of power over them, sell their younger brother into slavery in Egypt. There, after being falsely accused of attempted rape by the wife of his owner, and after spending some time in prison, Joseph rises to a position of power when he advises Pharaoh how to save his country from starvation. The cycle draws to an end during a period of famine, with Jacob and all his descendants emigrating from Canaan to Egypt. There, a forgiving Joseph arranges for their safety and sustenance.

The narrative concludes with Joseph's death and his brothers and their families remaining in Egypt. The second to last line of the cycle holds out a vague hope of better things to come in an uncertain future: "And Joseph had his brothers swear: God will indeed take account of you [here in Egypt, and when He does you will leave Egypt] and take my bones away from here" (Gen. 50:25). The stories in this large narrative block are divided in four parashiyot: Va-yeishev, Miqqetz, Va-yiggash, and Va-yehi.

At the end of the last cycle of stories in Bereishit, God's promises to Abraham, which have been repeated to Isaac and to Jacob, are far from being fulfilled. Abraham's descendants remain refugees from the drought in Canaan, a small group of foreigners living in Egypt under the protection of its king.

LITERARY THEMES

Bereishit contains four literary themes that repeat in different stories.

(1) The theme of the younger child supplanting the older is repeated obviously three times and gives rise to much of the drama in Bereishit: Isaac over Ishmael; Jacob over Esau; Joseph over his brothers. In each case, the older brothers all give rise to large groups of people: Ishmaelites/Arabs, Edomites, and ten of the tribes of Israel, respectively. Joseph's two sons, Ephraim and Manasseh, give rise to the

largest of the Israelite tribes. This theme is used to illustrate that God favors whomever he wishes. In each case, it is the younger son who unexpectantly becomes the important figure in the ensuing development of the story.

God's preference for Abel's offering over that of his older brother Cain, and Jacob's favoring of Rachel over Leah, her older sister and his first wife, are less obvious expressions of the same theme.

(2) The theme of the younger son in danger occurs three times in Bereishit: Abraham plans to kill his son Isaac; Esau plans to kill his brother Jacob; and the brothers plan to kill Joseph. In each of these cases, the threat to the younger son has the potential to affect the outcome of God's promises to Abraham, but in each case the threat is averted: God stops Abraham; Esau cools down after Jacob flees to Mesopotamia; and Judah talks his brothers into selling Joseph to Ishmaelites, descendants of their grandfather's brother.

(3) The theme of the barren ancestress occurs three times. Not only Sarah, but also Rebecca and Rachel are barren. Only after different types of intervention do they give birth to the very children that affect the destiny of Israel.

(4) Related to the preceding is the theme of an ancestress pretending to be the sister of her husband because her husband is thought to be in danger. In each case, the barren woman endangers herself and the lineage promised Abraham. As a consequence of her heroic lies, Sarah is taken into the harem of Pharaoh in Egypt and later into the house of Avimelech, King of Gerar (12:10-20; 20:1-18). Rebecca's lie exposes her as well to the danger of being taken into a harem in Gerar (26:1-11). In the first two stories, God's active, divine intervention saves Sarah; in the third, Rebecca is saved by a fortunate happenstance.

(5) The significance of courageous or resourceful women, though underemphasized in the narratives of Bereishit, is nevertheless mentioned. Of the twelve main human characters in Bereishit adumbrated above, six are women, two of whom are not ancestresses of Israel. Eve, the ancestress of humanity, is the person

who, motivated by her interest in wisdom (3:6), makes it possible for human beings to distinguish between "good and bad." Hagar, Sarah's Egyptian maidservant who had a child with Abraham and was mistreated by her mistress, is presented sympathetically, as a longsuffering individual. Showing his favor, God sent an angel to comfort and guide her, and later revealed himself to her. He tells her that the son she is carrying by Abraham will become a nation (16:6–16; 21:11–21). Within the lifetime of Abraham, Ishmael had twelve sons who gave rise to twelve tribes (25:12–17), foreshadowing the twelve tribes of Israel that would descend from Jacob.

LITERARY THEMES FROM BEREISHIT THAT CONTINUE INTO THE SUBSEQUENT BOOKS OF THE TORAH

The promise of overwhelming numbers of progeny made to Abraham and reiterated to Isaac and Jacob is fulfilled in the next section of the Torah, at the beginning of Shemot/Exodus. It is also in Shemot/Exodus where God describes his special relationship with the descendants of Israel, referring to them as "My firstborn son" and "My son" (Exod 4:22–23).

Allusions to the promises of progeny and land occur elsewhere in the Torah whenever the names Abraham, Isaac, and Jacob are employed together. This is a way of emphasizing that the first promise is fulfilled but not the second. In fact, the promise of land is fulfilled only in the books of Joshua and Judges, which follow the Torah.

The significance of the Sabbath, mentioned at the end of the first story of creation, is spelled out after the exodus from Egypt, even before the Israelites reach Sinai, but then again at Sinai. The rules of proper comportment and people's obligations vis-à-vis each other and with God are only implicit in Bereishit, for example, in the stories of Cain and Abel (Gen 4), the kings of the North and Lot (Gen 14), Lot and the people of Sodom, and Lot with his daughters (Gen 19). These rules are stated explicitly and in great detail in the following books of the Torah.

SOME THEOLOGICAL IDEAS IN BEREISHIT

Bereishit expresses its understanding of God by describing his actions as they affect the cosmos and humanity. In the following books of the Torah, additional ideas are introduced, and those listed below are developed and expanded. Some of these appear in Bereishit, but they are not dealt with in detail.

(1) God is unique. He creates the natural world, he commands, he blesses, and he promises.

(2) The culmination of God's creation of living creatures is the human being. Only humans and their descendants are created in the image of God.

(3) The world, after being thoughtfully and conscientiously created by God, may no longer be described as turbulent and chaotic (1:2). The cosmos, humanity included, is intelligible, comprehensible.

(4) God, who is always present in the world, covenants with people as he wishes – Noah and all humanity; Abraham and all his descendants – and punishes or forgives people when they have not behaved justly and in accord with moral principles. This is fair, because, since Adam and Eve ate from the Tree of Knowledge of Good and Bad (not Evil), they and all their descendants are capable of discerning good from bad, right from wrong.

(5) Broadly accepted social norms are perceived as good natural laws, governing proper behavior between humans, that have divine sanction. Therefore, since humans are capable of making ethical decisions about how to conduct their daily lives and manage their society, God holds them accountable for violating norms governing topics such as proper attire, sexual improprieties, misappropriation of property, homicide for no appropriate reason, and the fair adjudication of conflicts.

(6) God self-distances himself from people. In the beginning of human history he is intimately involved in supervising and reacting to the activities of humans and talks with them. In the Abraham-

Isaac cycle he appears only at crucial moments, while in the Jacob cycles he retreats even more. By the Joseph cycle, he is no longer actively involved in the drama. People, however, are able to discern his presence by interpreting events around them.

(7) The literary form of Bereishit is that of journalistic history. It presents events in chronological order, and, beginning with the Abraham Cycle in chapter 12, describes how one event gives rise to another in a logical, comprehensible sequence. Unlike modern histories, however, Bereishit does not move rapidly from story to story; rather, it slows its pace to present human-interest stories that reveal the inner character of its heroes: their strengths, passions, wisdom, and even their faults. In this way, Bereishit connects a unique past with a present that keeps changing depending on the social and intellectual location of those who read it. The use of narrative history – as opposed to outright mythology – to express beliefs about the origins of the cosmos and the founders of a community is unique among peoples of the ancient Near East. The choice of the genre of history-writing reflects a theological idea because the stories about Israel's ancestors are part of God's biography in the time-space continuum of human beings, busy with life's activities in a very real, material world.

Bereishit informs its readers that God existed always in the past – as did some primeval material stuff, such as water, darkness, and wind – indeed, even before the extant cosmos came into existence, and continues to exist in the present of those reading or hearing the narratives. He is the catalyst for many, if not all, significant events.

Consequently, by remembering and interpreting the past as presented in Bereishit, readers may determine what is useful for reflecting upon and understanding their own lives.

These theological notions are refined in the following books of the Torah. The last point is developed fully in Devarim/Deuteronomy, where Moses appears not as a prophetic figure delivering God's instructions – as in Shemot/Exodus, Va-yiqra/Leviticus, and Be-midbar/Numbers – but as a teacher. There, in the last section of the Torah, at the very end of Israel's wilderness period, when everyone from the generation that was with him at Sinai is dead except Joshua and Caleb, Moses interprets narratives about past events, as well as rules and laws, for those about to enter the land promised to Abraham's descendants. Moses teaches on his own authority. He is the prototypical teacher, responsible for educating the next generation. That is why he became known in rabbinic tradition as "Moshe Rabbenu," "Moses our teacher." He is not only the storyteller and lawgiver, but also the interpreter of these stories and laws, the ideal model for those who would teach Israel centuries later – the rabbis.

WHO WROTE BEREISHIT AND WHEN?

Bereishit does not name anyone as its author, but Jewish tradition maintains that Moses wrote it to provide background to the events that occurred in his lifetime as well as to the revelation of divine teachings that followed. This position, however, does not have to imply that Bereishit was revealed to him at Sinai along with instructions that he received there and elsewhere during the years of wandering. Moses could have heard the stories of Bereishit as family lore during the decades that he lived with his own people, and recorded them so that Israelites would always know who they were, from where they had come, and how it happened that their ancestors had been slaves in Egypt.

HOW JEWS READ BEREISHIT

Jews today read Bereishit from the perspective of their own time and place, but also from the perspective of their ancestors at the foot of Mt. Sinai more than three millennia ago. On the one hand, Jewish reading undertakes to comprehend the book as it was understood when first heard. This type of understanding was called *"peshat"* by medieval Jewish exegetes. *Peshat* refers to the straightforward or "plain" meaning of a text in its original language and literary, biblical context. (All translations into all languages try to render the *peshat*. Good translations, however, such as those of Richard Elliot Friedman, Robert Alter, and Everett Fox, undertake not only to render the *peshat*, but also to reflect the flow of the ancient syntax along with some echoes of the original Hebrew rhythms, rhymes, and word-plays.) But the *peshat* of Bereishit does not clarify its cultural meaning. That meaning has been provided for Jewish culture by interpreters of the text, beginning from the prophets who preached in ancient Jerusalem in the days of Solomon's Temple, through the medieval and modern rabbis, to contemporary scholars who teach in yeshivot, seminaries, and universities.

Introduction to Exodus

DAVID H. AARON

Hebrew Union College – Jewish Institute of Religion

THE FIVE BOOKS THAT COMPRISE THE TORAH TELL STORIES OF Israel's origins in two discrete developmental stages. The first book, Genesis, fosters ethnic identity by suggesting that all Israelites derive from Jacob and four women, Leah, Bilhah, Rachel, and Zilpah. As such, the primary emphasis of Genesis is the creation of a people through *endogamy*, that is, marriage among a distinct cluster of clans, all of which descend from Jacob, the son of Isaac, the son of Abraham. As for what distinguishes Israelite culture or religious practices from those of other Canaanite peoples, the Book of Genesis provides very few details. We learn that Abraham and his descendants were in a unique relationship with their God, called יהוה (commonly rendered, *Yahweh*, Gen 15:7), but the book is nearly silent regarding rituals, beliefs, and social customs that might have distinguished the Israelites from their neighbors. The authors of Genesis were concerned with creating a feeling of unity based on the concept of blood-relations. The notion of shaping group identity on the basis of life-practices was not part of their literary agenda.

The Book of Genesis ends with the Israelites forced to flee to Egypt in order to escape a famine. As such, Genesis ends with Israel in exile, setting the stage for the rest of the Torah's narrative. Save for a few chapters in Genesis, the events recorded in the Torah

---

* The content of this chapter appears with greater elucidation in David H. Aaron, *Genesis Ideology: Essays on the Uses and Meanings of Stories* (Eugene, OR: Cascade Books, 2017), chap. 14.

unfold in exile – first in Padan-Aram, then in Egypt, and finally, in the wilderness. The Torah's subsequent books, starting with Exodus, entail narratives that focus on the *content* of Israelite life and socio-political organization. While successful at integrating within Egyptian society during the lifetime of Joseph, son of Jacob, the story presents a degradation of living circumstances upon Joseph's demise. It is then that the general population is enslaved so as to undermine their ability to pose a military threat to the Egyptian monarchy.

Outside of the Hebrew Bible, there are no literary or archaeological voices corroborating the historicity of an Israelite enslavement lasting some 430 years (as suggested by Exodus 12:40); nor are there sources verifying a mass exodus of people as numerous as the Israelites allegedly were at the time of their redemption (see Exod 12:37, purporting an exodus of 600,000 men alone). Given that the story of Israel in Egypt was originally fashioned as an allegorical representation of the historical exile experienced by the writers' own generation, the search for an Egyptian sojourn will prove fruitless. The story of Israel in Egypt reflects the authors' strategies for generating cultural and religious identity as well as hope, so that their generation might be able to cope with an increasingly dispersed peoplehood. In its final state, the story crafted by Israelite scribes during the post-exilic period (after 538 BCE) constitutes a virtuosic achievement designed to do all that Genesis leaves incomplete: the creation of a literature that would generate cultural content and identity even in the face of a seemingly desperate state of defeat at the hands of Babylonian armies.

Israel in Egypt is the story of an oppressed people living far removed from a homeland, without the organizational structures enjoyed by all other autonomous ancient civilizations: a monarchy, a priestly caste with permanent cultic sites, and most importantly, a land of their own. How, then, might the people survive such circumstances? Exodus's authors answer this question by fusing together older literary traditions and images of the land of the Pharaohs with newly invented cultural solutions. Genesis had already stipulated that Abraham and his descendants could relate directly to their God without an intermediary, both in the land of Israel and in Mesopotamia (Padan-Aram). The Exodus authors further that ideological premise by integrating commitments to law, custom, and ritual into the God-People relationship. Reading Exodus, one comes to understand that God spoke to Moses for the first time in the wilderness – that the historical moment and the handing over of the tablets of the Decalogue to Moses did not occur at Mt. Zion in Jerusalem (cf. Isa 2:3), but rather took place in the middle of an uncharted desert which did not belong to any particular tribe or clan. Israel's great redeeming leader was not a king, but a man who merged the wisdom of a sage-teacher with the insights of a prophet bearing God's will. The underlying message of the entire narrative is at once simple and idealistic: if the Israelite people could survive the horrors of servitude under the whips of Pharaoh's taskmasters in antiquity, they can surely survive their present challenges of dispersion in Babylon and other lands. The story suggests that redemption by God was possible even in that most extreme of situations. No matter where the Jew is situated, God's voice can be heard and his hand in history felt. The allegory may have been situated in a remote time and place, but, for the post-exilic world, its lessons were the source of hope and perseverance, both within the homeland and in far-off lands.

Today's readers of Torah are often so acclimated to the biblical narrative that they might not recognize just how creative the Exodus narrative was in its own day, or how radical. Over the centuries, the allegory was literalized into "history," undermining the inventiveness of the book's authors. The destruction of Jerusalem, the loss of a monarchy, and deportation were all historical events for which we have much literary and physical evidence. The use of allegory permitted the authors to disguise their agenda and displace blame from the perpetrators who still held sway over Israel's destiny. In effect, they shifted the message of survival and redemption to the venue of an ancient Egyptian kingdom, which, during the writers' lifetime, no longer had significant political power.

The creation of Moses as a king-like prophet constitutes one of the Exodus writers' more ingenious innovations. Outside of the

Torah, many so-called early prophetic writings, such as those of Amos and Hosea, convey awareness of God's redemption of Israel from Egypt, but no pre-exilic Hebrew literature makes mention of Moses, Aaron, and Miriam.[1] The climactic scene of Moses's career, the giving of the Ten Commandments on stone tablets on Mount Sinai, is mentioned in no other biblical passage outside of the Torah, save for a single verse in 1 Kings (8:9) – a late, ideologically charged interpolation intent on dispelling the notion that God actually "lives" in the ark.

The present form of Exodus is the result of multiple stages of development, though the exact compositional history cannot be delineated. We recognize this by virtue of a number of story fragments that were obviously reshaped within the narrative by subsequent editors. For instance, in Exodus 4, when Moses asks God for a way to convince the Israelites that his authority derives from their ancestral deity, God provides Moses with a series of magic tricks. As the story unfolds, these magic tricks fail to appear in the scene introducing Moses to the Israelite slaves, but are instead revamped and integrated into Moses's first appearance before Pharaoh and his courtiers (chap.7). The failure of these tricks to impress Pharaoh provides the authors with the opportunity to exploit an extended story of divinely sanctioned plagues. In Exodus the plagues are ten in number (chaps. 7-12), but in Psalms 78 and 105, only seven are mentioned (with slightly different terminology for some plagues), likely representing an earlier stage of the story's development. Additionally, there are reasons to see the plagues as emerging somewhat in conflict with what might have been the originally planned redemption scene involving God's splitting of the Sea of Reeds before the charging Egyptian army (chap.15). The present story has two climactic scenes: that of the tenth plague,

---

1   Micah 6:4 reads, "I sent before you Moses, Aaron, and Miriam," but the date of this text cannot be determined. It is the only mention of the three siblings together outside of the Pentateuch. Jeremiah (15:1) pairs Moses with Samuel when speaking of Israel's heroic intercessors on behalf of the people before God. Moses appears in no other pre-exilic prophetic writing.

which results in the invention of the Passover Ritual, and that of the defeat of Pharaoh's army at the Sea. Both, however, accomplish the same thing: they demonstrate the power of Israel's God over the forces of history, both natural and human.

The plague narrative provocatively yielded the invention of the פסח, the *pesaḥ* ritual. The authors integrated what appears to have been an ancient practice of painting doorposts with blood to fend off evil spirits with the final plague, "death of the firstborn." The generic custom was re-mythologized, transforming what appears to have been a common apotropaic (protection) ritual into the specific act performed by Israelites on that very night to prevent the "Destroyer" (המשחית) from entering their households. Although the common rendering of the word *pesaḥ* is "Passover," in chapter 12 of Exodus the term unequivocally means "to protect," reflecting the apotropaic resonances of the ritual's original purpose. This is made explicit in the story: "For the Lord will pass through (עבר) to smite the Egyptians, but he will see the blood on the lintels and doorposts and *protect* (ופסח) the entrances, not permitting the Destroyer to enter into their [the Israelite] homes to smite [them]" (Exod 12:23).

The use of *matzah* as an aspect of the redemption scene is less elegantly integrated. Unleavened breads were a standard component of the sacrificial cult (see Lev 4:2, 13, 22, et al.). It is most likely the case that a celebration of springtime crops entailed special foods, some associated with the eating of slaughtered animals and others, perhaps, associated with the harvest itself. When *matzah* is first introduced in Exodus 12 there is no intrinsic relationship between the *pesaḥ* slaughter and the unleavened bread (12:15–20). The writer of the Book of Deuteronomy, who removed the practice of slaughtering an animal at the observer's home and made it an exclusively temple-oriented "sacrifice" (cf. Deut 16), emphasized *matzah* as the principal non-cultic observance of common Jews. The last part of Exodus 12 was eventually harmonized with Deuteronomy's notion that non-leavening flatbreads were consumed because there was insufficient time for the bread to rise on the night that the Egyptians cast Israel out of their land (see Deut 16:3). The notion that the breads could not rise (Exod 12:39) is in direct conflict with the overall intention of the chapter's first verses, which suggest that the animal used to protect Israelite homes was designated a full four days before the slaughter would take place, leaving plenty of time to prepare the meal adequately. Moreover, according to the *pesaḥ* aspect of the story, there could not have been a nighttime departure (as is suggested in Exod 12:31) given that the success of the ritual is predicated on the notion that the Israelites would remain within their homes until daybreak so as to take advantage of the divine protection afforded by the bloodstained doorposts. As modern readers, we should embrace these tensions within the story's evolution as suggestive of how diverse schools of thought struggled to shape Jewish practices. Today, Jews celebrate Passover with *matzah*, while the protective home slaughter ritual is only symbolically preserved by placing a lamb's shank-bone on the Seder Plate.

The Babylonian division of Exodus according to an annual reading cycle renders the book into eleven parashiyot or lections. European traditions stemming from the thirteenth century organized Exodus on the basis of some forty chapters. As noted, the book underwent stages of development. At its core is the story of Israel in Egypt (chaps. 1–14), which concludes with their crossing the Sea of Reeds (chap. 15). With the second part of chapter 15 (vv. 22–27) there commences a series of scenes that portray Israel's wilderness sojourn as fraught with stresses over leadership and survival. The wilderness sojourn becomes a repository for situating a variety of literary genres, each of which permits its authors to address questions of practice, belief, leadership structures, and identity. Many of these stories (in Exodus and Numbers) reinforce the authority of Aaron and his descendants as High Priests. Entire sections of Exodus (chaps. 25–31 and 35–40) address issues only of concern to the priesthood's cultic responsibilities.

The scene at Mount Sinai (chaps. 19–20) was not likely part of the book's original design, but it spawned some of the most significant religious symbols in the history of Judaism. In God's presence, Moses fashions a legal system with two types of documents. The first entails the fashioning of two stone tablets, symbolic of God's covenantal relationship with Israel as being founded upon a basic ethical code. The second part includes more extensive legal judgments, frequently referred to as "The Covenant Code" (Exod 21–24). Here again, we see imaginative innovation at work. The standard symbol of a covenantal agreement among many ancient Near Eastern cultures was the standing stone (מצבה). When Jacob is portrayed as establishing a border agreement between his clan and that of Laban, both men erect the equivalent of standing stones (Gen 31:46). Similar objects appear prominently in Joshua 4 (vv. 3, 8, 9) and 8:29. Such monuments were supposed to evoke awareness of covenantal relations between various parties, or alternatively, between a people and their God. For a diaspora community, the disadvantage of this symbol is that it is fixed in the ground where the covenant was first established and not where the people might be located. A symbolic stone erected at Mount Sinai, located far from Israel's desired homeland, could hardly have served its purpose of evoking remembrance of a heroic past. To accommodate the evocative nature of this symbol, the Exodus author invents the *portable stone tablet*, eventually to be housed and carried through the wilderness in the Ark of the Covenant. So as not to completely bypass the original symbol, Moses is also said to have erected twelve stones, one for each of Israel's tribes, at the end of his forty days on Mount Sinai (Exod 24:4). But these are distinct from the tablets that contain God's actual writing. The portable tablets reinforce the notion that God can establish a covenant of law with the Jews anywhere without foregoing the power implicit in the symbol of standing stones.

The content of the Decalogue is decidedly secular, save for one ethnically based religious commandment – observance of the Sabbath. The school responsible for the contents of the Decalogue was apparently sensitive to how Israelites might appear to other peoples, both within the region of Israel's homeland and in the diaspora. Thus, the Ten Commandments commence by stipulating Israel's unique relationship with a principal deity, which would have emulated how other peoples in the region would have expressed allegiance to their own local deities. The core of the commandments, however, is totally in harmony with what every other culture in the region valued: prohibitions against theft, murder, adultery, and behaviors thought to threaten sovereignty over property. The design of these commandments and the "Covenant Code" that follows were meant to suggest that the Israelites had achieved a level of civilization at least equal to those associated with law-giving monarchies dating back to the recesses of antiquity, the most celebrated being those of King Ur-nammu (twenty first century BCE), Lipit-Ishtar (nineteenth century BCE), and Hammurabi (eighteenth century BCE). The writers of Deuteronomy make this concern for achieving parity among the nations of the world explicit when they write that the laws will serve as "proof of [Israel's] wisdom and discernment to other peoples, who, upon hearing these laws will think, 'Surely this great people is a wise and thoughtful people'" (Deut 4:6).

Not every ideological school was enamored with the secular Decalogue that would find its way to Exodus 20. A counter-narrative was composed by priestly intellectuals who portrayed God's covenantal document quite differently. The story of the "Golden Calf" (Exod 32–34) depicts Moses destroying the initial tablets – symbolically representative of the "secular" Decalogue – when he witnesses the idolatrous (assimilationist) observances of the people who fashioned a surrogate for Moses's leadership during his forty-day absence on Mount Sinai. Going back up the mountain, Moses would ultimately deliver the version of the covenant that we read in Exodus 34. It is highly ethnocentric in character, commencing with a prohibition against assimilation amidst adjoining populations, which includes a stern condemnation of intermarriage and the production of idols (34:12–17). The edicts then continue with observance of the Matzah Festival (v. 18), dedication of the first-born to God (vv. 19–20), the observance of the Sabbath (v. 21), the Feast of Weeks (Shavuot, v. 22) and the other festivals as pilgrimage observances, etc. It is beyond the scope of this introductory essay to discuss why both versions of the Decalogue were preserved by the final editors of Exodus; what is clear, however, is that the book's editors regularly preserved various (even divergent) perspectives on Israel's formation, taking advantage of the core indeterminacy of all allegorical stories.

Based on practices already evident within the Torah, the exodus would become the paradigm for all discourse concerned with future redemption. Additionally, rituals that ostensibly had little to do with the original exodus "event" would be integrated into the dominant themes of the exodus – particularly, God's interaction as a historical force. As such, just as the *pesaḥ* slaughter itself was likely a generic apotropaic rite, the other pilgrimages ultimately associated with the exodus appear to have had their origins in agricultural practices, or, in the case of Sukkot, in an ancient Enthronement Ritual, cognizance of which is still preserved in the Mishnah Rosh HaShanah (1:1: "the first of Nisan is a new year for kingship and pilgrimages"). Similarly, the use of טטפות (*totafot*), or "amulets" on straps affixed to the forehead and arm was depicted as a normative heuristic device by the Deuteronomist for teaching future generations about God's law-based covenant (Deut 6:8; 11:18). The dominant imagery in those contexts is not the exodus from Egypt, but the origins of the covenant with Abraham, Isaac, and Jacob (Deut 6:10 and 11:21–25). In contrast, Exodus 13:16 associates the use of טטפות (*totafot*) with the Exodus story, noting that they are placed on the hand and forehead to evoke cognizance of Israel's deliverance from Egypt by "a mighty hand" (Exod 13:16). The Ashkenazic morning ritual of *tefillin* alludes to this verse ("וְשֶׁנִּזְכֹּר נִסִּים וְנִפְלָאוֹת שֶׁעָשָׂה עִמָּנוּ בְּהוֹצִיאָנוּ מִמִּצְרָיִם" / "Let us remember the miracles and wonders that [God] did for us when He took us out of Egypt").

Remembrance of the exodus from Egypt is a central element of principal liturgical components in the daily worship ritual, including the recitation of Exodus 15 prior to the morning "Call to Worship." In Exodus 20:11, Sabbath observance is justified as emulating God's desire for rest on the seventh day. This justification was not attractive to the Deuteronomist thinkers, who objected to anthropomorphic depictions of Israel's God. Thus, in Deuteronomy 5:15, Sabbath observance is justified as a remembrance of what it was like to have been slaves, working without rest. The later rabbinic sanctification of the Sabbath with wine draws upon both themes.

The dominance of the literary imagery of Exodus remained constant through the Second Temple period and into the Rabbinic Era, especially with the fashioning of Passover rituals in the Haggadah shel Pesaḥ. Each Jew was to imagine having participated in the redemption experience of the ancient Israelite, fostering a constant empathy for those whose lives were oppressed, and inspiring hope in all Jews who would imagine a return to the Promised Land.

Introduction to Leviticus

ALAN COOPER

Jewish Theological Seminary

THE BOOK OF LEVITICUS/VA-YIQRA CONSTITUTES THE CENTER of the Torah both literally and figuratively. As the third of the five books, it forms the literal center. Moreover, according to a report in the Babylonian Talmud, Kiddushin 30a, the ancient scribes who "counted all the letters of the Torah" determined that the midpoints of the Torah in letters, words, and verses, respectively, were to be found within Leviticus. The literal centrality of Leviticus, however, is far less consequential than its figurative significance. The book is the primary source for four concepts that are foundational for biblical religion and undergird post-biblical Judaism as well: the offering of *sacrifices* as the principal system of worship; the *priesthood* as the sole legitimate form of religious leadership; ritual *purity* as a necessary condition for participating in religious activity; and *holiness* as the ideal state both of individuals and of the community as a whole in relation to God.

Those concepts serve as organizing principles for the book, which is mostly straightforward and lucid in composition. The four themes are italicized as they appear in the following outline:

Chapters 1–16: Priestly Torah

- 1–7: Instructions for occasional *sacrifices* (exclusive of calendrically fixed offerings; cf. especially Leviticus 23 and Numbers 28–29 for the latter)
    - 1:1–2: introduction

- 1:3–5:26: whole offerings, gift/tribute offerings, well-being offerings, purification ("sin") offerings, reparation ("guilt") offerings
- 6–7: additional details and instructions

• 8–10: Narratives about successful and unsuccessful ritual performance

- 8: consecration of priests and Tabernacle (sequel to Exodus 28–29; 40:12–15)
- 9: inauguration of cult
- 10: ritual failure, followed by conclusion of initiation rites

• 11–16: Instructions about purity

- 11–15: manifestations of impurity
  ◦ 11: animals (food)
  ◦ 12: childbirth
  ◦ 13–14: skin eruptions and related conditions
  ◦ 15: genital discharges
- 16: purgation of impurity

Chapters 17–26: Holiness Code

• 17–22: Rules and prohibitions relating to holiness

- 17: animal slaughter for food
- 18: illicit sexual relations
- 19: rules for maintaining holiness
- 20: illicit sex and other forms of profanation
- 21–22: prohibitions specific to priests and sacrifices

• 23–25: Regulations pertaining to sacred times and other holy things

- 23: festivals
- 24: various holy things, including the divine name
- 25: sabbatical year, jubilee, release from indebtedness

• 26: concluding blessings and curses

Chapter 27 – Appendix (commutation of obligations to the sanctuary)

The Book of Leviticus assumed its present shape as a result of editing and rewriting over the course of several centuries. Two distinct strands of priestly ideology may be discerned within it. The earlier is contained within chapters 1–16, which seem for the most part to be a literary recasting of a manual of practical guidance for priests. These chapters codify various priestly responsibilities and prerogatives – the divine instruction for priests known as "priestly *torah*" – for the edification of a non-priestly audience. The text conveys some of the information that priests require in order to exercise their sacerdotal functions as cultic officiants, and to fulfill their pedagogical duty to "distinguish between the holy and the profane, and between the pure and impure" (10:10).

While the sacrificial laws are based on descriptive ritual texts, they are overlaid with a prescriptive veneer that integrates them into the narrative of the Sinaitic revelation (see 1:2; 4:1–2; 5:14; 5:20, etc.). The text does not take up the meaning of sacrifice or explain why it should be the preferred form of worship; those matters are left open to interpretation on the part of both the participants in the rituals and the readers of the texts. The beginning of Leviticus – "When any of you brings an offering" – presumes spontaneous motivation on the part of the worshippers. As Jacob Milgrom comments, "The common denominator of the sacrifices discussed in these chapters is that they arise in answer to an unpredictable religious or emotional need."[1] Sacrifices may be occasioned by feelings of gratitude or guilt, or they may fulfill specific cultic requirements for achieving expiation, reparation, or purification. The sacrificial cult supports the sanctuary and its operatives, offers opportunities for commensality – a vital means of cementing social bonds – and most importantly, restores and sustains the proper relationship of both individuals and the community with God.

In Leviticus, priestly authority is conferred entirely and exclusively on the Aaronids ("Aaron and his sons," a phrase that occurs more than sixty times in Exodus and Leviticus; see especially Exod 28:1; 40:12; Lev 8:2, 6). There is no hint of the struggle over altar rites

---

[1] *Encyclopaedia Judaica*, 2nd ed., vol. 12 , p. 735.

that surfaces in the Qoraḥ rebellion (Num 16). The priests serve as intermediaries between the Presence of God in the Tabernacle and the outside world. Their charge is to perform the sacrificial rituals with punctilious accuracy, and their failure to do so can have disastrous results, as exemplified in the admonitory account of the deaths of Aaron's sons, Nadav and Abihu, in Leviticus 10:1-11. While it is not certain what the "strange fire" was that they brought before God, it is clear that it was something that God had not commanded (10:1). God met their fire with a fire that "came forth and consumed them" (10:2). Commentators have derived many lessons from the story, but at its heart it is about an antinomy that is inherent in religion: proximity to God offers the prospect of both great blessing and terrible destruction. The work of the priests is essential but it also is fraught with danger; strict observance of the law is the only way to mitigate the danger and bring about the blessing. As it is for the priests, so it is for all Israel, which is why the priests are enjoined to "teach the Israelites all the laws" commanded by God and transmitted by Moses (10:11).

In order to guard against contamination that could engender destruction, the priests must maintain the Tabernacle in a state of ritual purity, allowing only objects and persons that are ritually pure to enter into proximity to God. The concept of ritual purity is part of a bipolar scheme that divides everything into the categories of clean/pure (*tahor*) and unclean/impure (*tame*). The usual glosses of the underlying Hebrew words can be misleading, since the operative concepts have more to do with normalcy and deviance, respectively. For humans, deviance is defined by conditions that compromise the integrity of the body (deformities, afflictions, emissions). While the particular notions of what is normal and what is deviant may be at odds with modern sensibilities, taken on their own terms they constitute a coherent system. Should the *tame* come into contact with the Holiness of God, the result would be "profanation" of God, with dire consequences.

Since the human body is "in the image of God," according to the priestly author of Genesis 1:27, it too must be protected from profanation (cf. Lev 11:44-45). The living must avoid contact with the dead, and the flesh of "unclean" animals must not be ingested. The criteria that distinguish "clean" from "unclean" animals may not make sense to modern readers, but once again, they appear to operate according to certain standards of normalcy and deviance. For example, edible fish are defined a priori as having fins and scales (11:9). Fish-like animals that do not possess those two characteristics are deviant, and may not be consumed. Likewise, animals that live in the water but move about on legs (like crabs and lobsters) and birds that cannot fly clearly are deviant, and may not be eaten. Ethical considerations also may be a factor in rendering animals unfit for consumption, as in the prohibition of carnivorous beasts and birds of prey.

The priestly author of Leviticus marks the collection of purity laws in chapters 11-15 as a digression from the book's narrative flow. Leviticus 16:1 begins with the words, "The Lord spoke to Moses after the death of the two sons of Aaron," picking up a thread that was dropped following the report of the ritual failure in chapter 10. The intervening laws concerning dietary restrictions (chap. 11), childbirth (chap. 12), skin eruptions and related afflictions (chaps. 13-14), and bodily emissions (chap. 15), seem to stand outside the story's time. Aside from their concern with purity and impurity, what those laws have in common is that they address the essential characteristic of human existence, the fact of *embodiment*.

In traditional Jewish thought, embodiment and mortality are the principal factors that distinguish humans from God. In his "Laws of Repentance" 3.7, Maimonides condemns as a heretic anyone who conceives of God as having bodily form. Unlike God, human beings must take in sustenance (chap. 11) and reproduce (chap. 12) in order to survive, and they inevitably endure physical corruption (chaps. 14-15) and death. Those are characteristics of humanity, natural concomitants of embodiment. The laws of personal purity provide a means of bridging the seemingly unbridgeable gap between the human and the divine, to make human life more "holy" despite its innate limitations. Most imitative of the divine ideal are the rites of Yom Kippur, when worshippers symbolically divest themselves of embodiment, purging themselves of physical need and desire for a single day of "complete rest...and self-denial" (Leviticus 16:32) each year. It is a purifying experience, and also a vivid reminder of human frailty and imperfection.

In the later stratum of Leviticus (chaps. 17–26), the sphere of holiness that must be protected is extended beyond the precincts of the Tabernacle to encompass the entire world. Leviticus 19:2 sounds a clarion call when God commands Moses, "Speak to the whole community of Israel and say to them: 'You shall be holy, for I, YHWH your God, am holy.'" The emphasis on "the whole community" marks a departure from the priestly *torah* of the earlier chapters, and the idea that the entire community is in some sense "holy" moves away from the notion that the Tabernacle is the singular venue of holiness.

In ancient times, the term "holy" (*qadosh*) was glossed as "separate, distinct." As applied to God, the term was understood to denote God's utter uniqueness; as applied to Israel, it was taken to mean that Israel was distinguished from other nations because of its special relationship with God ("a priestly kingdom and a holy nation," according to Exodus 19:6; see also Leviticus 20:26). This notion of holiness as "separateness" often persists in later times, although different commentators have varying notions of what it means. There are those who discern some qualitative difference between Israel and the rest of the world; others say that what is distinctive about Israel is that God chose Israel as the vehicle for conveying God's word to all of humanity. Some suggest that since God is incorporeal, all people should strive to purge themselves of worldliness and corporeality insofar as it is possible to do so. Others react against that idea and say, rather, that "holiness" is maintained by steering a middle course between the extremes of abstemiousness and hedonism.

All of those interpreters assumed that Leviticus 19:2 was drawing an analogy between God and the community, thereby suggesting that people should attain to holiness by imitating God in some manner. More likely, though, the verse uses the word "holy" in two different senses. In the first sense, "holiness" denotes the essential characteristic of deity. It is an abstract term, in contrast to the "glory" (*kavod*) of God, which is the tangible presence of God in the world. In the second sense, "holiness" signifies a relationship of nearness to God, which is an equivocal thing. On the one hand, God's Presence may bring great blessing to the community; on the other hand, nearness to the Presence makes it incumbent for the community to maintain itself in a state of purity or risk destruction. And that onus is no longer placed exclusively or even primarily on the priests, but on every single Israelite.

The sphere of holiness, in this later view, extends far beyond the confines of the Tabernacle. A glance at the laws in Leviticus 19–21 shows how holiness encompasses every aspect of human behavior, including not only cultic matters but also civil law, ethical behavior, agricultural practices, and more. The sequence of laws in chapter 19 is revealing in its randomness: honoring parents, keeping the Sabbath, not making idols, not consuming the meat of a sacrifice for more than two days, leaving the edges of a harvested field for the poor, refraining from theft, deceit, false oaths, coercion, withholding wages, and so on.

Almost every one of those laws concludes with the statement, "I am the Lord," or "I am the Lord your God," which denotes the fact that God is omnipresent, and not merely resident in the Tabernacle. Perhaps most characteristic is Leviticus 19:14: "You must not insult the deaf, or place a stumbling block before the blind. You shall fear your God: I am the Lord." Lest anyone think that it would be a simple matter to get away with tripping a blind person, the law serves as a stern reminder that there is always at least one witness to every human action – God. Failure in such ethical matters, no less than failure to maintain oneself in a state of ritual purity, profanes the holiness of God, and the consequence is that "the land to which I bring you to settle in will spew you out" (20:22).

The Torah mandates continual human effort to conform to the divine ideal while recognizing the deficiencies that are inherent in the human condition. The laws of Leviticus provide both cultic and behavioral means of compensating for those deficiencies. The priestly *torah* regulates specific human activities and situations that can impede communion with God within the cultic sphere: eating, reproduction, sexual activity, bodily afflictions and emissions. The Holiness Code expands the strictures beyond the requirements of cult to include all sorts of human endeavors with particular emphasis on ethics and social welfare. Some of the ethical elaborations of the Decalogue in Leviticus 19 are at the heart of Western morality: "Love your fellow as yourself" (19:18) is a prime example.

Both the language of the priestly laws and many of their details require updating and reinterpretation if they are to retain their relevance. The disjunctions between ancient and modern thought are undeniable, and in some cases there may be no way to resolve them. Gendered aspects of purity and impurity that made sense within the priestly system, for example, are problematic in a culture that values sexual equality. Adherents to traditional Jewish liturgy continue to recite prayers for the rebuilding of the Temple and the restoration of its cult. Productive reinterpretation is evident in the fact that for the past two millennia, the prayers themselves along with intensive study of the sacrificial laws have served as meaningful surrogates for the actual performance of sacrifices. While some Jews proudly claim descent from Aaronid and other Levitical lines – and a few outliers are preparing themselves for service in a rebuilt Temple – even prior to the destruction of the Second Temple religious leadership was passing from the hereditary priesthood to a meritocratic rabbinical class. Finally, while in the absence of a Temple most of the laws of purity are dysfunctional, it is not hard to discern their persistent effect on cultural attitudes towards gender and sexuality, dietary regimens, and health and hygiene. Although ritual purification is no longer attainable in accordance with the laws of Leviticus, one can purchase a facial cleanser called "Purity Made Simple," manufactured by Philosophy, inc.!

Introduction to Numbers

JACOB L. WRIGHT

Emory University

Following the Jewish tradition, the third book of Moses, Leviticus, is named after its opening word: Va-yiqra, "and He [the Lord] called." In contrast, the fourth book of Moses is not named after its first word: *Va-yedabbeir*, "and [the Lord] spoke." Instead, the book is called Be-midbar, "in a desert" (not "in *the* desert"). Be-midbar is the fifth word of the book, where it is immediately specified to mean the "Sinai Desert." In contrast to its simple title, Be-midbar is rich in complexity. Indeed, it is itself a wilderness of sorts, through which many generations have wandered without ever fully managing to grasp its contours.

Following the long lists of laws and rituals in Va-yiqra, a narrative is set into motion when we reach Be-midbar. Israel now strikes out to cross the desert and take possession of the Promised Land. The story begins with Israel at Sinai and ends with the people "in the plains of Moab, by the Jordan at Jericho," where the process of settlement begins. On the way to this final destination, new commands and decrees are revealed to Moses.

The blend of legislative and narrative content in Be-midbar is reminiscent of the book Shemot/Exodus. However, the rich diversity of content and genres represented in Be-midbar makes this text unique among the books of the Torah. Be-midbar includes

Translated from the German by Alisa Rethy.

poetry, quotations from other books, descriptions of legal disputes, itineraries, records, laws and directives, war reports, death announcements, etc. Its varied nature reflects the complex history of its composition.

In recent scholarship on the Torah, Be-midbar occupies a central point of interest since it presents exceptionally complex issues. Some scholars, especially in Israel and the USA, still work with the "four-source" hypothesis, or the Documentary Hypothesis, attributing the entire contents of the book to the sources known as the Jahwist, the Elohist, the Deuteronomist, and the priestly source (although the Deuteronomist is normally not identified in this particular book). In contrast, European research has largely given up this approach for several decades now. However, a new consensus has not been reached, and viewpoints differ widely: on one side, many claim that the book is simply a later insertion into the Torah. On the other side, some insist (justifiably) that the book contains both very new and very old material.

When God promises in Exodus 3:8 to lead Israel out of Egypt and into "a good and spacious land," the reader also expects to hear about the execution of this promise. That report can be found in the Book of Joshua, and the connecting links between Exodus/Shemot and Joshua appear in both Be-midbar/Numbers and Devarim/Deuteronomy. The report of Miriam's death in Numbers 20:1 likely belongs to the oldest parts of Numbers, along with the statement in 22:1: "And the Israelites then marched on and encamped in the plains of Moab, across the Jordan from Jericho." This is the place where Moses gives his farewell speech in Deuteronomy and from which he ascends to the summit of Mount Pisgah to die. The statement in Be-midbar 25:1, "While Israel was staying at Shittim," is undoubtedly a part of the same literary core. Shittim is the starting point for the settlement of the land in the Book of Joshua (Josh 2:1; 3:1).

All of these texts are difficult to explain as late additions. In fact, Be-midbar provides the missing links of an ancient (pre-exilic) Exodus-settlement narrative.

In nineteenth- and twentieth-century research, many exegetes tried to locate the original oral traditions behind the literary configuration. Today, this approach is only undertaken in exceptional cases. Most exegetes have correctly recognized that, for example, the registers in Numbers 1–4 do not trace back to early sources but, rather, are late (largely post-exilic) constructions and include highly developed political interpretations. However, one can also find a number of passages that belong to older literary contexts. The poetic text in Numbers 21:27–30 resembles passages of the Book of Jeremiah, while Numbers 21:14 cites from the Book of the Wars of the Lord (apparently an anthology of poems describing the victories of the Lord over Israel's enemies). These citations from older sources create an antique impression. According to Robert Alter, though, creating this impression is a conscious choice of the authors. Alter refers to this phenomenon as the "antiquity effect" (drawing from Roland Barthes' concept of *"effet de réel"* or "reality effect").

ISRAEL IN THE DESERT

Be-midbar has a decidedly military, if not militant, character. Why is this the case? Is the reader being encouraged to lead a militaristic existence? Probably not. Rather, this presentation of Israel's early history serves to convey statements about the people's condition during an entirely different epoch – namely, the period directly preceding and following the downfall of the Judean Kingdom and the loss of military power in 586 BCE.

Accordingly, the war camp of the Israelites in Be-midbar is analogous to the culture of the warship in Herman Melville's short novel *Billy Budd*. Both are used as models of society through which the authors approach a broad variety of questions regarding such issues as authority, social class, national unity, relationships to neighbors, integration of outsiders, etc. The hostile populations inhabiting the desert represent the kingdoms that later forced the people of Israel and Judah out of their land, scattering them into the diaspora.

In Be-midbar, Israel begins its march from Sinai through the desert to take possession of Canaan. But after the spies turn back with "an evil report," the people refuse to take possession of the Promised Land and, as a result, are punished by God. Thanks to the intervention of Moses, Israel is spared total annihilation. However, an entire generation is condemned to die in the desert; only their progeny are permitted to see the Promised Land.

This punishment is undoubtedly among the latest elements of the book. Many passages in Be-midbar, and also especially in Devarim, appear unaware of its existence. But why was it added?

Be-midbar addresses each new generation of Israel. The post-exilic communities that identify with the nation must learn from the experiences in the desert. Due to its unbelief, Israel could not enter the Promised Land, and saw an entire generation perish. Now, like then, Israel must submit to the authority of Moses (meaning, the authority of the Torah) in order to survive the dangerous wilderness and finally reach its homeland. The people must not doubt the power of their God. The divine presence must be able to dwell in their midst. Their priests and Levites must be able to fulfill their divinely ordained tasks. The people must obey the purity laws and steer clear of pagan temptations. And all must work toward the unity of Israel.

THE UNITY OF ISRAEL

Immediately at the beginning of the book, in Numbers 1-2, the ideal unity of Israel is illustrated through a census of the population. It is structured around the twelve tribes; all political, territorial, and societal disparities are leveled. Israel is one people, not because a ruler merged together various groups and regions, but because all of its members share the same ancestors. (As a result, the question of outsiders is frequently addressed.) The census begins with Reuven, not because his future territory is of greater value, but because he is Jacob's first-born son.

The sons of Aaron and the Levitic clans perform special duties that they won for themselves after protracted political struggles (during the monarchy and then after the exile). However, Be-midbar

(Num 3–4) provides an entirely different reason for their status, tracing it to the divine decree given to their ancestors.

After addressing the duties of these special classes, the book presents laws pertaining to non-priests (Num 5–6). The sequences of these laws suggest that preserving the holiness of Israel is not only the responsibility of the priests. The entire nation dwells with the Mishkan (the Tabernacle) in the camp, and therefore all members of the community must abide by strict purity laws. By taking the special vow of the Nazirite, even ordinary Israelites – men as well as women – can devote themselves to God (Num 6).

The chiefs of the tribes bring sacrificial offerings for the consecration of the altar (Num 7). The offerings consist of bowls/plates, sprinkling bowls, basins, etc., which in the ancient Near East were otherwise only offered by the king and his court. In this way, Bemidbar transfers royal powers to the entirety of the population.

Social hierarchies are spatialized in this book. As Naḥmanides and others have observed, the portable Mishkan replaces Sinai as the holy site where God is encountered and divine laws are communicated. Many of the prohibitions concerning Sinai are transferred to the Mishkan: the Israelites must keep their distance from it and must not dare to gaze at the divine presence. The camp is a prototype for the ideal form of Israel's society: "The Lord is in their midst as at Sinai in holiness" (Ps 68:18). In Va-yiqra, the human body occupies the position the camp occupies in Be-midbar: skin, for example, corresponds to social borders, and skin disorders mark threats to those borders. Rabbi Judah Halevi combines both models by comparing the camp to the body and designating the Mishkan as the heart of this body.

QUESTIONS OF AUTHORITY, FAITH, AND TRUST

The first part of the book concludes in chapter 10 with the establishment of the camp, the departure from Sinai, and the arrival in the desert of Paran. Various themes intertwine in the next chapters, and the tone changes markedly: in chapters 1–10, Israel is unified in its obedience, but now, as Israel leaves Sinai, this unity gradually disintegrates. Questions of authority, faith, and trust emerge as central themes in these texts.

First, Moses demonstrates his function as intercessor (Num 11). Through his mediation, he manages to bring God not only to lift his punishment, but also to provide his people with the meat for which they had long been yearning. The reader should keep these things in mind when encountering the Israelites' unbelief in the following chapters.

After God transfers a part of his Spirit from Moses to the elders of Israel, Miriam and Aaron raise their voice against their brother. In response, God proclaims the specific quality that sets Moses apart: in contrast to the prophets, with whom God communicates in visions and dreams, God speaks with his "servant" from mouth to mouth, and not in riddles. Moses's singular authority, distinguished from Aaron's and Miriam's, matches the authority of Moses's Torah over both priestly (Aaron) and prophetic (Miriam) institutions. Since Be-midbar is directly beholden to priestly influences, this message stands out and is reiterated throughout the book in different ways.

The narratives in chapters 12–20 deal with the same themes of faith and authority: an entire generation is condemned to die in the desert as a result of their unbelief (Num 13–14). Laws are revealed pertaining to cases of intentional and unintentional disobedience (Num 15). A Levite named Qoraḥ incites a rebellion against Moses and Aaron, together with Datan, Aviram, and two hundred fifty chiefs of the congregation (Num 16:3): "You have gone too far! For all the community are holy, all of them, and the Lord is in their midst. Why then do you raise yourselves above the Lord's congregation?" This rebellion, in turn, incites an uprising of the entire congregation (Num 17). The authority of Aaron and of the priests is then confirmed, and their role is emphasized in the important purification ritual, the *parah adummah* (Num 18–19). At the end of this section, though, even Moses and Aaron fail to honor God and are condemned to die before the Israelites take possession of the land (Num 20).

These episodes showcase the unique relationship between God

and Moses. Following the incident with the spies, for instance, God wants to strike Israel with pestilence and make a greater and mightier nation out of Moses alone (!) (Num 14:12). But in his humility, and cleverness, Moses makes use of a shrewd argument to turn God away from this plan (14:15–16): "If then You slay this people to a man, the nations who have heard Your fame will say, 'It must be because the Lord was powerless to bring that people into the land He had promised them on oath that He slaughtered them in the wilderness.'" In response God decides to forgive Israel.

ISRAEL'S RELATIONSHIP WITH OUTSIDERS

From chapter 20 onward, the subject matter and tone of the book change once again. Be-midbar now focuses on Israel's relationship with outsiders and its position among the nations. Accordingly, the nation's disobedience and unbelief no longer occupy the foreground.

Chapter 20 voices a polemic against Judah's southerly neighbors, the Edomites. The authors report that the Edomites had no sympathy for Israel, their brother nation, when Israel returned from Egypt to its homeland. They forbade the Israelites from passing through their territory, engaging their armies against them. With the construction of this "memory," the authors aimed to demonstrate that Edom had been hostile toward Israel from the very beginning. The polemical tone of this report stands in sharp contrast to Jacob and Esau's reconciliation in Bereishit (Gen 33).

The wars with Sichon and Og are similar to the confrontation with Edom, but have an entirely different function. When Sichon and Og refuse passage, Israel does not retreat as in the case of Edom. Instead, Israel subjugates both kings and takes possession of their territories. The great victories in the region east of the Jordan are meant to spur Israel on toward Canaan, and Moses repeatedly recalls these successes in his war sermons in Devarim.

Israel's military triumphs culminate with the lengthy story of Balaam. Here, there is no war to report, since the land of Moab (and Ammon) was never intended to be occupied by Israel. Rather, this triumph is to be found in the words of the non-Israelite prophet Balaam, whom the Moabite king had paid to curse Israel. Such punishment of enemies through a curse belongs to ancient Near Eastern wartime conventions, and a seer with the name Balaam even appears in an Aramaic inscription found in Jordan, dating from the ninth/eighth century. As the biblical story progresses, instead of cursing Israel, Balaam's beautiful speeches promise rich blessings for the nation's future. This is the source of the well-known verse: "How fair are your tents, O Jacob / Your dwellings, O Israel!"(Num 24:5).

Directly following these three chapters comes the unfortunate report that Israel has begun to "whore" with the daughters of the Moabites (and Midianites). God's wrath breaks out in the form of a plague, striking down 24,000 Israelites. But, thanks to the intervention of Pinḥas, a descendant of Aaron, the plague is stopped. Because he "took impassioned action for his God, thus making expiation for the Israelites," God rewards Pinḥas with a "pact of friendship" and secures for his descendants "a pact of priesthood for all time" (Num 25:12–13). Here, a priestly family has written itself into Israel's history, justifying its high status by appeal to a memory of martial activity on the deity's behalf. At this point, the portion of the book treating Israel's relationships to outsiders concludes with a new census (Num 26).

THE LAND

The final portion of the book focuses on the land of Israel which a new generation now has in its sight. The chapters in this section are framed on both ends by a legal case presented by the daughters of Zelophehad (Num 27:1–11 and 36:1–12), after which the contents of the entire book are summarized in Be-midbar's final line: "These are the commandments and regulations that the Lord enjoined upon the Israelites, through Moses, in the fields of Moab, at the Jordan near Jericho" (Num 36:13).

Be-midbar emphasizes Israel's unity and equality. Special emphasis is placed on the point that the land has to be divided fairly amongst the nation's tribes and families. The story of a man (Zelophehad) who dies without male heirs illustrates this point. After this man's death, his five daughters announce their intention to inherit their father's land. Moses brings the matter to God, who finds favor with the daughters and enacts a new permanent law in response to their complaint. This is the only time in the Torah that a law is enacted in response to a human initiative, and remarkably that initiative is undertaken by women.

Following the creation of this new law, the themes of death and land are addressed further. God commands Moses to climb the mountain, from whose summit he will gaze upon the Promised Land and then die. It is at this point that Joshua is ordained as Moses's successor.

Chapters 28–29 connect space with time: God sets out the schedule for the daily, weekly, monthly, seasonal, and yearly sacrifices that Israel must offer from the harvests of the land. What follows is a description of women's vows, but their relationship to the context is unclear. The victory over the Midianites, which would be out of place earlier in the book, is reported here because the census of the new generation presents a caesura in the narrative. Alongside the sacrificial laws, these passages also address issues of atonement and reconciliation.

The region east of the Jordan plays a major role in Be-midbar. The victories over Sichon and Og anticipate the triumph in Canaan. If the Jordan marks the border of the land, what is to become of the population that lives east of the river but identifies itself with Israel? Do they belong to the nation? The authors approach this question in chapter 32, which tells how two-and-a-half Israelite tribes settle in the region east of the Jordan yet still agree to take the vanguard in the wars for their "brothers" on the western side of the Jordan. This episode illustrates what defines a member of Israel: obedience to the divine command spoken through Moses along with solidarity with the nation in difficult times.

After a description of the route from Egypt to Moab which God commands Moses to record (Num 33), God issues special battle orders: the Israelites are to expel all the inhabitants of the land, destroy their religious practices, and divide the territory fairly among themselves. The borders are clearly described (Num 34); Israel should take possession only of this region and never succumb to the temptation to expand its borders as empires do. Cities are now set apart for Levites, who do not inherit land with the other tribes, as well as for those who commit involuntary manslaughter: "You shall not defile the land in which you live, in which I Myself abide, for I the Lord abide among the Israelite people" (Num 35:34).

Introduction to Deuteronomy

BERNARD M. LEVINSON

University of Minnesota

DEUTERONOMY/DEVARIM MAY WELL BE THE FIRST BOOK TO POSE the problem of modernity. Its authors struggled with issues conventionally viewed as exclusively modern ones, such as the historical distance between past and present, the tension between tradition and the needs of the contemporary generation, and the distinction between divine revelation and human interpretation. Seen from this perspective, ancient Israel's Deuteronomy becomes a remarkably contemporary text, one that challenges its readers to rethink their assumptions about time, about Scripture, and about religion. Of course, Deuteronomy is also a deeply traditional text that, more than any other book of the Bible, provides the foundation of Judaism. The religious conviction that God made a covenant with Israel at Sinai, and that the Torah embodies the terms of that covenant, is fundamental to Deuteronomy. Many familiar Jewish ritual objects, like the *mezuzah*, the *tefillin*, and the *tzitzit* (fringed garment), are, in part, based on Deuteronomy, as is Judaism's most important prayer, the Shema (6:4–9). But the Shema is more than a prayer. Judaism understands its recitation to be a binding legal act in which individuals pledge their commitment to God. By reciting the Shema, the congregation in the synagogue brings the plot of Deuteronomy to life in the present, as it enacts and renews that oath of allegiance to God that, it believes, Israel first vowed on the plains of Moab.

The story begins just as the Israelites, encamped on the plains of Moab, stand poised finally to enter the Promised Land. The entry into Canaan would provide the long-awaited climax of the story that had begun with the promises to the ancestors in Genesis, and whose fulfillment had been delayed by the enslavement in Egypt and the wandering in the wilderness. Now, on the eve both of his death and of the nation's entry into the land without him, Moses, portrayed as Deuteronomy's speaker, arrests the narrative action in order to deliver a series of three speeches, grouped together as a long valedictory address. He reviews the nation's history, expounds upon their laws, and instructs them about the importance of loyalty to God. He also adjures the nation, from the plains of Moab, to uphold this combination of law and theological instruction as a covenant, one that supplements the covenant previously sworn at Horeb (the name for the mountain of revelation, called Sinai elsewhere; 28:69). Only after the conclusion of these discourses and a following appendix (chaps. 31–34) does the overall narrative line resume with the account of the nation's entry into Canaan in Joshua and Judges.

THE HISTORICAL CONTEXT AND LITERARY BACKGROUND

The second word of the book, "Devarim," "[the] words," gives the book its most common Hebrew title, following an ancient Near Eastern convention of naming books after their opening phrase, or incipit. In contrast, the standard English name of the book, "Deuteronomy," goes back to the Greek Septuagint (to *deuteronomion*, yielding Latin Deuteronomium), meaning "Second Law." That approach to naming the book represents the Greek translation of the Hebrew phrase "Mishneh Torah" found in Deuteronomy's Law of the King, where it refers to "a copy of the law" (17:18). That phrase was understood in ancient rabbinic sources as a reference to the Book of Deuteronomy itself (Sifre Deuteronomy §160), understood as a "second law" or "repetition of the law," because of the extent to which Moses, throughout the book, revisits the earlier laws and narratives of the Tetrateuch (the first four books of the Bible) and teaches Israel about them (see Naḥmanides on Deut 1:1 and Ibn Ezra on Deut 1:5).

Despite the literary attribution of the text to Moses as its speaker, from the vantage point of modern biblical scholarship Deuteronomy more likely arose in its present form at a later period of Israelite history. The main sections of the book fit best in the seventh century BCE, as the composition of educated scribes associated with Jerusalem's royal court. It has been long recognized that there are very striking similarities between the distinctive religious and legal requirements of Deuteronomy and the account of the major religious reform carried out by King Josiah in 622 BCE. That reform had been inspired by the discovery in the Temple of a "scroll of the Teaching" (Heb. "Torah"; 2 Kings 22:8). Josiah's reform restricted all sacrificial worship of God to Jerusalem and removed foreign elements from the system of worship (technically, the "cultus"); it culminated in the celebration of the first nationally centralized Passover at the Temple in Jerusalem (2 Kings chaps. 22–23). So strongly do these royal initiatives correspond to the distinctive requirements of Deuteronomy that scholars have long identified the "scroll of the Teaching" discovered in Josiah's Temple as Deuteronomy, and thus have assigned the book a seventh-century date.

Josiah's reform, with some form of Deuteronomy as its catalyst, was much more a revolution than a simple return to older forms of worship, as the Book of Kings suggests. Previously, it was entirely legitimate to sacrifice to God anywhere throughout the land, as did Abraham at Shechem and Bethel (Gen 12:7–8); Jacob at Bethel (Gen 35:1–7); Samuel at Mitzpah, Ramah, Gilgal, and Bethlehem (1 Sam 7:9, 17; 9:11–14; 10:8; 16:1–5); and Elijah upon Mount Carmel (1 Kings 18:20–46). Indeed, even earlier biblical law, associated with the revelation at Sinai, stipulated that God would grant blessing "in every place where I [God] cause My name to be mentioned" (Exod 20:21). Deuteronomy challenged that older norm, prohibiting sacrifice "at any [or, every] place" and restricting it to a single site, understood to be Jerusalem (Deut 12:13–14). It is therefore striking that Deuteronomy presents itself as both an explication of the prior covenant (1:1–5) and as a supplement to it (28:69). Deuteronomy justifies itself in two ways, yet neither description acknowledges the extent to which Deuteronomy actually challenges and revises earlier law.

The historical background of Josiah's reforms was the increasing threat of imperial domination. The Northern Kingdom of Israel had fallen under the Neo-Assyrian invasion a scant century before (722 BCE; 2 Kings 17). Continuing Assyrian incursions down the coastal littoral had all but reduced Judah to a rump-state (2 Kings 18:13). In a desperate bid to preserve the nation's autonomy, Hezekiah had already made a pact with Assyria (2 Kings 18:13–18). Subsequently, Judah's political and religious independence seemed to hover uncertainly between the threats presented by Assyria and resurgent Babylon (2 Kings 20:12–15). The resulting military allegiances led to religious syncretism, as Judean officials introduced various foreign forms of worship into the Temple (2 Kings 16:10–20; 21:1–6).

In this context, Josiah's religious reforms represented an important bid for Judean cultural, political, and religious autonomy. The monarch extended his reforms into the area of the former Northern Kingdom of Israel and thus implicitly into territory under Assyrian control (2 Kings 23:15–20). Deuteronomy, apparently written sometime during this historical crisis, likewise reflects the desire to preserve Judean cultural and religious integrity. Its authors had the conviction that older conventions of worship and social organization were no longer viable. If the religion of YHWH was to survive the crisis, renewal and adaptation were necessary. Deuteronomy's legal corpus (chaps. 12–26) provides a comprehensive program for cultural renewal. It addresses worship, the festival calendar, the major institutions of public life (justice, kingship, priesthood, prophecy), criminal, family, and civil law, and ethics. The law is presented as a covenant between God and nation, which the people take an oath to uphold, upon penalty of sanctions, while maintaining unconditional loyalty to their God. That covenant structure closely corresponds to the Neo-Assyrian state treaties that have been recovered from this period, the most famous of which is the Vassal Treaty of Esarhaddon (672 BCE). At a number of points, the authors of Deuteronomy seem consciously to have patterned their covenant after this treaty tradition, which they could have known either directly or in Aramaic translation. From this perspective, Deuteronomy represents a counter-treaty: its authors turned the weapon of Assyrian imperialism into a bid for Judean independence, shifting its oath of loyalty from the Assyrian overlord to their divine sovereign.

Thus tutored in international treaty conventions, the authors of Deuteronomy elsewhere reveal their knowledge of two additional important literary genres from the ancient Near East: the legal collection and wisdom literature. The laws in 15:1–18, 17:8–13 and 14–20, and 22:13–23:1 all contain elements of ancient Near Eastern law codes or legal practices that have been transformed to bring them into alignment with Deuteronomy's religious priorities, especially its goal of centralization and purification of worship (chap. 12). Similarly, Deuteronomy's emphasis on wisdom (1:13; 4:6; 16:19) and its admonition not to alter the Torah (4:2; 13:1) echo motifs also found in biblical and extra-biblical wisdom literature. Moreover, the scribes responsible for Deuteronomy employed a convention of authorship familiar in their time. They did not directly attach their name to their composition or write in their own voice. Instead, they attributed their composition to a prestigious figure from the past. By employing "Moses" as their spokesperson, they established a link with tradition at precisely the time when tradition, for the sake of survival, had to be transformed. This convention of ascribing a text to an ancient personage, called "pseudepigraphy," is well known in the literature of the Second Temple period; examples include Jubilees, 4 Ezra, the Testament of Abraham, and (among the Dead Sea Scrolls) the Temple Scroll.

THE LAYERS OF TRADITION

Deuteronomy preserves several layers of tradition: the structure of three different discourses with an appendix already suggests a process of literary growth. That growth is closely connected to the gradual formation of the Hebrew Bible. To appreciate what is involved, it helps to imagine the time before there was an assembled, complete Bible as we now know it.

1. When Deuteronomy was first promulgated, it would not have

been part of any larger whole. Instead, it would have stood by itself as a "scroll of the Torah" (i.e., the "scroll of the Teaching" in 2 Kings 22:8). It would have consisted primarily of some form of most of the laws of chapters 12–26, framed by a relatively simple introduction and conclusion. This form of Deuteronomy presented itself as a treaty concluded between the nation and its God in a formal ceremony whereby each citizen took an oath of loyalty under penalty of strict sanctions (28:1–46). This was very likely the pre-exilic form of Deuteronomy.

2. At a later stage, presumably sometime during the exile (586–538 BCE), Deuteronomy would have been incorporated into the Deuteronomistic History (Joshua through 2 Kings) to serve as its introduction. At this point, the "Deuteronomistic" editors would have given the book its present literary frame (1:1–4:40, chaps. 31–34), while also adding to the legal corpus, selectively tying its promises or expectations to the later historical material. Expansions in Deuteronomy that reflect the Babylonian exile may derive from this stage (i.e., 4:25–31; 28:47–56; 30:1–10).

3. At a still later point, in the post-exilic period, priestly editors appended Deuteronomy to the nascent Torah, to serve as its conclusion. Ironically, the decision to conclude the Pentateuch with Deuteronomy interrupted and delayed the overall narrative plot of Genesis through Numbers, which reaches its climax in an account of the conquest of the land. This narrative climax was delayed until Joshua.

The placement of Deuteronomy between the larger literary units of the other Pentateuchal material and the Deuteronomistic History makes an important theological statement. The Pentateuchal story of the promise of the land to the patriarchs, the enslavement in Egypt, the exodus, and the wilderness wandering now ends with Moses's death in Deuteronomy's last chapter (chap. 34), which brings to a close both the book and the Torah. But that formal conclusion now separates not only Moses, but also the reader, from access to the land whose covenantal promise was the point of departure for the entire narrative (Gen 12:1). Early on, from the vantage point of the Judean hills, Abram viewed the panorama of that Promised Land, as it extended in every direction of the compass (Gen 13:14-17). But, at the end of his life, he was constrained to bargain for a small plot of land where he might bury his wife, Sarah (Gen 23:1-20), poignant testimony that Abraham never gained full possession of the land promised him. So too now, closing the circle, does the Torah conclude with a panorama that symbolizes dislocation and loss, as Moses looks out over Canaan from the heights of Mount Pisgah. Prohibited from entering the very Promised Land to which he successfully led his people, he finds his only access in that forlorn prospect. Like Abraham, Moses saw the Promised Land stretched out before him, but he would never possess it. Looking into the land from the outside without possession of it thus forms a literary and theological inclusio[1] for the Pentateuchal narrative.

As with Abraham and Moses, so, too, the reader. Ancient editors have deliberately defined the Torah as a literary unit so as, first, to accommodate the addition of Deuteronomy and, second, to sever it from its logically expected fulfillment. The possession of the land is diverted instead into the next literary unit, which is to say, into the future. So profound a reconfiguration both of the patriarchal promise and of the overall plot is conceivable only in light of the historical experience of exile, which profoundly called the possession of the land into question. Had possession of the land remained central to the covenant during the exile, Israelite religion would have collapsed. By concluding the Torah with Deuteronomy and not Joshua, the fulfillment of the Torah is defined as obedience to the requirements of covenantal law rather than the acquisition of a finite possession.

THE TRANSFORMATION OF DEUTERONOMY IN THE SECOND TEMPLE PERIOD

In biblical narrative, "this book of Teaching" (Torah) crosses the symbolic geographic divide of the Jordan, carried, in the Ark of the

---

1 In biblical studies, a literary device which consists of placing similar material at the beginning and end of a section.

Covenant, upon the shoulders of the Levitical priests (Deut 31:25-26; Josh 3:14-17). So did the text of Deuteronomy cross the historical divide of the Babylonian exile, borne on the shoulders of the multiple Jewish communities that survived the exile and that developed their distinct identities thereafter. This crucial transition from the First Temple to the Second Temple periods, from pre-exilic Israelite religion to post-exilic Jewish religion, represents a major pivot in the history of Israelite literature, thought, and belief. The wrenching force of that transition, as institutions and assumptions underwent profound transformations, created "stress fractures" in the text of Deuteronomy. In many cases, pre-exilic religious and legal norms became unintelligible to these post-exilic communities. Therefore, in the process of teaching and translating Deuteronomy, they were forced to translate not only the language of the text but also its ideas: from one language into another, from one historical period into another, from one set of assumptions into another. Sometimes this overlay of post-exilic ideas may interfere with understanding the original meaning of the text, even though that overlay now represents the conventional way that Deuteronomy has come to be read and understood.

As a broader model for understanding such issues, it is helpful to view the religion of Israel reflected by Deuteronomy in the pre-exilic period as in many ways a "Near Eastern" religion. This applies preeminently to the original theology of the text, which, like all religions of its time and place, viewed its god as presiding over a "divine council" of lesser deities. From this perspective, texts like the second law of the Decalogue (5:7) and the Shema (6:4-9) called for exclusive loyalty to God, without thereby denying the existence of other deities, just as Near Eastern treaties required that a vassal swear allegiance to a single political monarch. But once radical monotheism became the Jewish norm in the Second Temple period, under the influence of exilic prophecy, the original "Israelite" view gradually became "foreign" and unintelligible. The Shema could only be understood as affirming the later "truth" of Jewish monotheism.

The same issue applies to law. In certain cases, the pre-exilic authors of Deuteronomy clearly followed Near Eastern procedures. For example, they required the immediate, summary execution of those disloyal to God, as if under the emergency conditions of martial law (13:10). In the Second Temple period, however, this breach of Deuteronomy's own requirement for due process (17:2–7) was understandably seen as inconsistent with the norms of Jewish law! The text was therefore read and taught as if the requirement for execution were to take place only after the due process that, in fact, it originally bypassed. As a next step, this originally oral legal interpretation of the law was introduced into the text of the law, when Deuteronomy was translated into Greek for the Jewish community of Alexandria (in the Septuagint, ca. 225 BCE). The conscientious translator could do no less, since that revision of the law was what the law "had" to mean!

Just as the Septuagint later updates the Hebrew in light of the Jewish law of its time, elsewhere the reverse may hold true. On occasion, the Greek version retains classical views of pre-exilic Israelite religion that have been updated or corrected in the standardized Masoretic Text of the Bible. For example, a comparison of the Hebrew text of verses 32:8 and 32:43 with the corresponding verses in the Septuagint and Dead Sea Scrolls suggests the Hebrew text has been altered to remove references to other deities. The authentically Israelite religious language seems to have become so alien that the Hebrew text was "corrected" to bring it into conformity with later Jewish theology. In such cases, the Septuagint or the Dead Sea Scrolls may open a window into the original meaning of a passage that has been lost in the Masoretic Text. It is important to remember, though, that these additional versions are themselves part of Jewish history. Because the Septuagint was later accepted as the Bible of the Church, it is often no longer recognized that it was a Jewish translation, prepared for the thriving Jewish community of Alexandria. In translating the Bible into their living language of Greek, that community saw the Torah as also telling their story. Thus, where Deuteronomy's Hebrew refers to the "horror" of foreign invasion as punishment for national wrongdoing, the Septuagint reinterprets that punishment as the contemporary experience of "diaspora" (28:25). The multiple Judaisms of the Second Temple period each had their own way of reading Deuteronomy, and thereby of understanding themselves as being addressed by Moses in his oration.

RABBINIC INTERPRETATION OF DEUTERONOMY

With the close of the biblical period, the entire Pentateuch (now including Deuteronomy along with the other, originally independent laws and narratives) came to be seen as a unified "Torah" that derived from divine revelation, mediated through Moses. For all subsequent religious communities that read it, the Torah represented a coherent and self-consistent document of utmost religious significance. Thus, the various inconsistencies that historical-criticism[2] would later point to as signs of the literary growth of the Pentateuch were interpreted in different ways by the ancient synagogue. For the rabbis, every detail of the biblical text was significant, and every redundancy, inconsistency, or contradiction had a didactic purpose. These phenomena are explained in rabbinic interpretation as important measures of the divine status of the Torah and as opportunities to draw out enriched meaning from the biblical text.

The Decalogue, which appears in two somewhat different versions in the Pentateuch (Exod 20:2–14 and Deut 5:6–18), provides a valuable example for demonstrating the creativity and theological richness of rabbinic hermeneutics. The Sabbath commandment in Exodus 20:8 instructs the reader to "remember" the Sabbath day, while Deuteronomy 5:12 requires the reader to "observe" it. Historical-critics regard these verses (and the Decalogues in which they are found) as two divergent traditions, each with its own social location and compositional history. Rabbinic interpretation, on the other hand, treats the two verses as variant records of the same event. God at Mount Sinai is understood to have proclaimed both "'observe' and 'remember' in a single utterance" (b. Shevu'ot 20b).

---

2   Criticism in the light of historical evidence.

That formulation, stressing the miraculous nature of divine revelation, remains part of the weekly liturgy in the beautiful Kabbalistic song, "Lekhah Dodi," sung at dusk as part of the Kabbalat Shabbat service, welcoming the sabbath.

Rabbinic exegesis takes a similar approach in order to solve a confusing problem with the narrative frame of Deuteronomy's Decalogue. The text is inconsistent regarding whether God spoke directly to the people (5:4) or only through the mediation of Moses (5:5). In addition, Deuteronomy's Decalogue contains an abrupt change from first-person to third-person reference to God (vv. 6-10 vs. 11-18). Historical-critics see these inconsistencies as evidence of different compositional layers, but the rabbis resolved these problems by suggesting that God Himself spoke only the first two commandments directly to the people, while Moses conveyed the rest to them on behalf of God, because the people complained that they were afraid of God (b. Makkot 24a; b. Horayot 8a).

The rabbis also applied their hermeneutical techniques to repetitions and inconsistencies in the detailed stipulations of biblical law. Historical-criticism explains variations in legal requirements between Exodus, Leviticus, and Deuteronomy, by attributing them to different law collections. As with the two Decalogues, each law collection had its own social location and compositional history. Rabbinic exegesis, on the other hand, often finds explanations for these issues by treating biblical law as case law: each repetition or inconsistency applies to a different case under the law. For example, they argue that the manumission laws apply to different types of slaves. Since Leviticus 25:39-46 specifically mentions debt slavery (v. 39), manumission in the Jubilee year applies only to debt slaves. Exodus 21:2-7, on the other hand, says "when you buy a Hebrew slave" (v. 2), so the rabbis conclude that the six-year term of service required in those laws applies only to Hebrews sold into slavery for stealing (Mekilta on Exodus 21-22). The stipulation in Deuteronomy 15:13-14 that slaves should be given gifts when they are freed, an issue not mentioned in either Exodus 21 or Leviticus 25, is then interpreted to apply to both of the above cases of Hebrew slaves, as well as to the case of the female Hebrew slave (Sifre

Deuteronomy 119). Thus, three different sets of manumission stipulations are understood to form a single, coherent system of manumission law. The examples provided here demonstrate just a few of the ways in which rabbinic exegesis – faced with a unified, divinely revealed, theologically coherent Torah – applied creative interpretive approaches to explain what historical-criticism would later understand as important evidence for the literary growth of the Pentateuch.

DEUTERONOMY'S CONTRIBUTION TO WESTERN POLITICAL THOUGHT

An overlooked chapter in the history of constitutional thought begins with the legal corpus of Deuteronomy. Although Western political theory is normally traced back to ancient Athens, and the concept of "separation of powers" specifically to Montesquieu's *The Spirit of the Laws* (1748), this standard model fails to take into account the contributions of ancient Israel to Western political thought. Deuteronomy's laws regarding public officials (16:18–18:22) are remarkable for providing what seems to be the first blueprint for a constitutional system of government. The jurists responsible for writing its utopian laws put into place two cornerstones of Western legal tradition: the clear division of political powers into separate spheres of authority; and the subordination of each branch to the authority of the law. Moreover, these visionary thinkers sought to safeguard the rule of law by establishing an independent judiciary. The carefully thought-out plan is designed to ensure that no single branch of government and no single religious institution should have sole power. Each is brought into relationship to the others and, more importantly, each is made subordinate to the one true authority: the law of Deuteronomy. Even institutions that might justifiably claim absolute authority – whether political, as in the case of the king (see Ps 2:6–7), or religious, as in the case of the prophet (see Exod 3:10–12) – are integrated into Deuteronomy's comprehensive vision.

The political experiment represented by Deuteronomy was

without precedent either in the Near East or in ancient Israel itself. It went far beyond what was strictly necessary as a consequence of the centralization of worship to the Temple in Jerusalem. The new constitution would have completely restructured the Judean polity (including the court system, the monarchy, and even traditional religious institutions like the priesthood and prophecy). In purely pragmatic terms, this utopian bid for freedom was a tragic failure.

Historically, there was simply no opportunity for it ever to be implemented. Upon the return from exile, when Judah regained some measure of political autonomy under Persian rule, internal conflicts over leadership of the polity and the cult between return-ees and those who remained in the land during the exile preempted this blueprint.

DEUTERONOMY AND THE CONTEMPORARY READER

Deuteronomy rewards the attention of contemporary readers and thinkers, whether religiously committed or secular, whether Jewish or non-Jewish. The modernity of Deuteronomy is that it does not permit itself to be read literally or passively. It challenges its readers actively to confront the problem of the relation between divine revelation and human interpretation, even as it breaks down the conventional boundaries between Scripture and tradition. It makes paradox central to its structure. As the book narrates the story of its formation, it also anticipates its prior existence as a complete literary work (cf. 29:26 and 31:9-13, 24-29). Interpretation is directly and indirectly a theme of Deuteronomy. At many points, the authors of Deuteronomy reinterpret earlier laws and narratives. Moreover, the process of the book's editing intentionally preserves conflicting perspectives on a full range of key issues central to Israelite religion: on whether the revelation of the Decalogue at Sinai/Horeb was direct or required the mediation of Moses (cf. 5:4 and 5:5, also discussed above); on the stature of Moses relative to other prophets (cf. 18:18 and 34:10); on the nature of divine punishment for sin (cf. 5:9-10 and 7:10); on whether God rules as head of a pantheon or is the only God who exists (as discussed above);

and even on Deuteronomy's own setting in time and place (cf. 1:1, which indicates Moses is speaking prior to the conquest, with 2:12 and 3:11, which contain information written from a post-conquest perspective). As with many other biblical texts, there is no facile "air-brushing" away of this interplay of perspectives, which reflects an ongoing ancient debate about fundamental religious assumptions. There is finally, for Deuteronomy, no access to God in the covenant without joining this debate. The reader of Deuteronomy must become, like the authors of Deuteronomy, an interpreter.

THE STRUCTURE OF DEUTERONOMY

I. The first discourse of Moses (1:1–4:43)
   A. Editorial headnote (1:1–5)
   B. Historical review (1:6–3:29)
   C. Exhortation to obey the Torah (4:1–40)
   D. Appendix: cities of refuge in Transjordan (4:41–43)

II. The second discourse of Moses (4:44–28:68)
   A. Introduction (4:44–49)
   B. The revelation of the Decalogue at Sinai/Horeb (5:1–30)
   C. Preamble to the laws: the requirement of loyalty to God (6:1–11:32)
      1. Validation of Mosaic instruction as revealed upon Horeb (6:1–3)
      2. A sermon on the first commandment of the Decalogue (6:4–25)
      3. The war of conquest (7:1–26)
      4. The temptation to pride and self-sufficiency in the land (8:1–20)
      5. The already broken and renewed covenant (9:1–10:11)
      6. Obedience as the condition for prosperity in the land (10:12–11:32)

D. The legal corpus (12:1–26:15)
  1. Centralization and purification of sacrificial worship (12:1–13:1)
  2. The requirement for unconditional loyalty (13:2–19)
  3. The obligations of holiness (14:1–29)
  4. Remission of debts and manumission of slaves (15:1–18)
  5. Sacrifice of firstlings (15:19–23)
  6. The festival calendar (16:1–17)
  7. Laws of public officials (16:18–18:22)
     a. The organization of justice (16:18–17:13)
     b. The law of the king (17:14–20)
     c. The Levitical priesthood (18:1–8)
     d. The Mosaic prophet (18:9–22)
  8. Cities of refuge (19:1–13)
  9. Boundary markers (19:14)
  10. The integrity of the judicial system (19:15–21)
  11. Rules for waging holy war (20:1–20)
  12. Atonement for an unsolved murder (21:1–9)
  13. Miscellaneous criminal, civil, and family laws (21:10–25:19)
  14. Concluding liturgies (26:1–15)

E. Formal conclusion: the reciprocity of the covenant (26:16–19)

F. Ceremonies at Shechem upon entry to the land (27:1–26; cf. 11:29–32)

G. The consequences of obedience or disobedience: blessing or curse (28:1–68)

III. The third discourse of Moses: the ratification ceremony for the covenant on the plains of Moab (28:69–30:20)

  A. Editorial heading: the relation between Moab and Horeb (28:69)

  B. Didactic review of Israel's history (29:1–8)

  C. Imprecation to ensure loyalty to the covenant (29:9–28)

  D. Reassurance of restoration (30:1–10)

  E. The accessibility of Torah (30:11–14)

  F. The necessity of choice (30:15–20)

IV. The death of Moses and the formation of the Torah (31:1–34:12)

    A. Moses makes arrangements for his death (31:1–29)

    B. The Song of Moses (31:30–32:44)

    C. Double conclusion to the Song (32:45–47)

    D. Moses commanded to die (32:48–52)

    E. The Blessing of Moses (33:1–29)

    F. The death of Moses (34:1–12)

Introduction to the Haftarot

LAWRENCE A. HOFFMAN

Hebrew Union College – Jewish Institute of Religion

THE HAFTAROT (SINGULAR, HAFTARAH) DERIVE THEIR NAME from the Hebrew root, *p.t.r*, "to take leave, dismiss, or conclude," making them the "concluding" readings of the Sabbath and Holiday lectionaries. Unlike the Torah readings that precede them, they are drawn from what Jews call the Prophetic Books (*Nevi'im*) – both the literary prophets and the books that describe the historical milieu of ancient Israel from the entry into Canaan (Joshua and Judges) to the first monarchic period in which the prophetic voice emerged (1 and 2 Samuel, 1 and 2 Kings). The connection between the haftarah and the Torah reading that it follows can be something of a mystery, but, in general, the haftarah continues a theme from the Torah portion – as, for example, the first day of Rosh HaShanah (the new year) when the Torah reading describes God's visit to Sarah to announce her imminent pregnancy (Gen 21), and the accompanying haftarah, which reports Hannah's petition to bear a child (1 Sam 2).

The opening three weeks of the Jewish lectionary are illustrative. The first column, below, provides the name of the Sabbath, drawn from the Torah reading; the others provide the Torah and haftarah readings with their opening words. Discussion follows.

Name of Weekly Reading	Torah Reading	Opening Line of Torah Reading	Haftarah Reading	Opening Lines of Haftarah Reading
Bereishit ("In the Beginning")	Gen 1:1–6:8	"In the beginning, God created the heavens and the earth."	Isaiah 42:5–43:10	"Thus said God, the Lord, who created the heavens and stretched them out, who spread out the earth and what it brings forth."
Noaḥ ("Noah")	Gen 6:9–10:32	"This is the line of Noah"	Isaiah 54:1–55:5	"Shout O barren one, you who bore no child."
Lekh Lekha ("Go forth")	Gen 12:1–17:27	"And the Lord said to Abram, 'Go forth from your native land.'"	Isaiah 40:27–41:16	"Why do you say, O Jacob, why declare, O Israel, 'My way is hid from the Lord?'"

The first case, Bereishit, is crystal clear. The Isaiah passage reiterates both the theme and the language of God creating the heavens and the earth. Noaḥ is less obvious. There is no parallel wording at all in the opening lines, so the synagogue worshiper hearing the portion must understand the larger context, in which Isaiah is comparing Babylonian exile to the devastation of the flood. Only in verse 54:9 do we hear explicitly, "This to Me is like the waters of Noah. As I swore that the waters of Noah nevermore would flood the earth, so I swear that…. My loyalty shall never move from you nor My covenant of friendship be shaken."

The opening words for the haftarah of Lekh Lekha also lack immediate resonance with the Torah portion, but verse 41:8 addresses Israel as "Seed of Abraham… whom I drew from the ends of the earth and called from the four corners." The message is that just as Abraham was summoned to the Promised Land, so too will the exiles be redeemed from captivity.

In only one of the three examples (Bereishit) does the opening line of the haftarah mirror the way the Torah reading begins, and here, the parallelism is relevant to the overall theme that the two readings share. Sometimes, however, the parallel between haftarah and Torah lections is verbal, but not thematic. The Torah reading Ḥayyei Sarah ("The life of Sarah," Gen 23:1–25:18), for example, deals primarily with Sarah's burial and the selection of Rebecca as Isaac's wife. But the search for Rebecca occurs because "Abraham was now old, advanced in years" (verse 24:1), a circumstance that suggested the haftarah of 1 Kings 1:1–31, which begins, similarly, "King David was now old, advanced in years." In content, however, the Kings passage (which chronicles the details of court intrigue) seems unrelated to the parallel Torah account of Abraham.

This rather chance correlation of wording without an obvious parallel of intrinsic theme is commonplace – another example is the haftarah prior to the new moon. The Jewish calendar reckons months according to the lunar cycle, so that the Sabbath prior to each new moon features a haftarah known as *maḥar ḥodesh* (1 Samuel 20:18–42), a name drawn from its opening line where Jonathan tells David, "Tomorrow will be the new moon [*maḥar ḥodesh*]." Aside from this chance calendric reference, however, the haftarah has little to do with the pending new moon. Its theme is the budding relationship between David and Jonathan, the new moon setting being distinctly secondary.

Our example of the first three weeks in the Jewish year suggests other lessons as well. To begin with, the readings here are all from Isaiah, and indeed, Isaiah is over-represented in the haftarot selections. Also, Ashkenazi and Sephardi Jews frequently differ in haftarah choices – the haftarah supplied here for Noah is Ashkenazi only; Sephardi Jews read Isaiah 54:10.

Variety in choice goes back to the very beginning, when two methods of reading Torah were normative. While Babylonian Jews from the third century on practiced the annual cycle that has become standard practice today, Jews in the land of Israel (medieval Palestine) followed what is loosely called a triennial cycle, whereby the Torah was read from beginning to end over the course of some three-and-a-half years. We saw above how the first reading for the annual cycle stretches from the story of creation (Gen 1:1) to the story of Noah (Gen 6:9). In Palestine of the same period, that first section (Bereishit) was subdivided into four separate readings, so that one reached the tale of Noah only in the fifth week. Our Isaiah reading that fits Genesis 1:1 accompanied just the first of the four readings. The other three had their own haftarot, which matched the lessons of the other three Torah readings – week two, for example, began with Genesis 2:4, "Such is the story of heaven and earth when they were created." The overall theme of its accompanying haftarah, Isaiah 51:6–15, seems relatively unrelated, but its opening words, "Raise your eyes to heaven and look upon the earth," echoed "Such is the story of heaven and earth."

The ancient Palestinian cycle of readings lasted until the First Crusade, when Jews fled crusading armies and remained largely absent from the land of Israel throughout the century-long duration of Crusader rule. By the time they returned, they had adopted the custom of the societies where they had fled, including the annual cycle of readings, which they brought back with them. The triennial cycle, and its accompanying system of haftarot, thus became a historical footnote.

Even the triennial cycle, however, had alternatives. Palestinian authors of synagogue poetry from (roughly) the fifth to the seventh centuries regularly embedded quotations from the triennial haftarot in their poetry, and these quotations have been compared to the listing of haftarot in genizah fragments, somewhat later in time (ca. ninth c. at the earliest); these also reflect Palestinian custom in the pre-Crusade era. The evidence from Yannai, one of the best known of these poets (ca. fifth century), regularly corresponds to the genizah material, even though other poets of the same era reflect different usage.

If, however, we use the genizah fragments and Yannai as our basis, we can see that many of the haftarot do continue themes of the Torah lections (as in the examples given from the annual cycle, above), but that others simply replicate opening words without an immediate connection (like the example from Isaiah 51:6–15, above). The triennial haftarot were also relatively tiny, compared to what we have today – usually 5 to 11 verses in length. Finally, Jews in antiquity saw the prophets as guaranteeing consolation born of the knowledge that even though God punishes Israel for its sins, God's love will ultimately triumph and Israel will receive divine redemption from the trials and tribulations of history. Intended, first and foremost, to provide this consolation (*n'chemta*), haftarah selections always end positively, to the point where the ancient Palestinian selections sometimes skipped several verses in order to reach a verse that might serve as a properly hopeful conclusion.

We mentioned above that Sabbaths receive names based on the lectionary: Shabbat Bereishit, Shabbat Noah, Shabbat Lekh Lekha, and the like. In this way, the spirit of the lectionary pervades the entire day. Indeed, the entire week is known by the same name, so that Shabbat Bereishit may mean either the Sabbath on which Genesis 1:1–6:8 is read, or the week that culminates in the very same reading.

But sometimes, the title is drawn from the haftarah portion, thus allowing the message of the haftarah to dominate the feeling and tone of the week in question. These haftarah-dominated titles tend to announce calendric occasions of particular consequence. Shabbat HaGadol ("The Great Sabbath") for example – the Sabbath prior to Passover – features a haftarah from Malakhi 3:4–24, which promises, "I will send the prophet Elijah to you before the arrival of the *great* [!] and awesome day of the Lord" (Malakhi 3:24). Special haftarot are assigned to all holidays as well. In the Middle Ages, even an upcoming wedding elicited such a haftarah – the so-called "Haftarah of the Groom" – probably, Isaiah 61 ("I will certainly rejoice"), but possibly also, 2 Samuel 22, David's praise of God for delivering him from destruction.

Sometimes, a series of haftarah readings over several weeks in succession define the character of the period leading up to or away from a holiday. The ninth day of the Hebrew month of Av (Tisha B'Av), for example, commemorates the destruction of both the first and the second Temple. Over time, Jewish imagination added other catastrophes to that day as well: the expulsion from Spain in 1492, for example. Traditionally, such tragedies have been seen theologically as punishment for sin, so that the period approaching Tisha B'Av has been overlaid with a sense of heavy foreboding. The immediate three weeks prior are called *bein hametzarim*, a colloquial phrase from Lamentations 1:3 implying "being in a tight spot." All of this theological apprehension comes through in the three haftarot of the period called *t'lata d'puranuta*, "the three haftarot of punishment." They culminate in the Sabbath immediately prior to Tisha B'Av, Shabbat Ḥazon ("The Sabbath of Vision"), from the haftarah of Isaiah 1:1–21, where the prophet confronts the "sinful nation" of Israel (v. 14) with his "vision" (*ḥazon*, verse 1:1) of God's punishment: "a land laid waste and cities burnt down, a wasteland consumed by strangers" (1:7).

As Tisha B'Av is preceded by the *t'lata d'puranuta* and their message of punishment, so, too, it is succeeded by a string of seven prophetic portions called the *shiv'ah d'n'chemta*, "The seven of consolation," which tradition reads as a divine-human dialogue. The first is Shabbat Naḥamu ("The Sabbath of Consolation") named for Isaiah 40:1–26, with its opening call (verse 1), *Naḥamu, naḥamu ami*, "Comfort ye, O comfort ye My people!" The next six haftarot, all of them from Isaiah, picture Israel and God debating the validity of God's promise from Shabbat Naḥamu, but concluding (with week seven) that in "love and compassion" (Isa 63:9), God has truly become Israel's "deliverer" (63:8).

This happy conclusion that God is ultimately loving and forgiving is particularly timely, because the very next week is Rosh HaShanah, the new year dedicated to repentance and pardon. The "seven haftarot of compassion" are thus not only a concluding bookend to the "three haftarot of punishment," carrying worshipers through the period from Tisha B'Av to the new year; they also frame the new year itself as a time of love, pardon, compassion, and deliverance – not just for Israel corporately, but for individuals who have sinned and require deliverance as much as Israel the People once did. These "seven haftarot of consolation," moreover, are followed by two more, known as *tartei d'tiyuvta*, "the two haftarot of repentance." The first of these is for the Fast of Gedaliah, falling just after Rosh HaShanah – an occasion not generally observed by non-Orthodox

Jews; but the second – Shabbat Shuvah, the Sabbath of Repentance, between Rosh HaShanah and Yom Kippur – is universal, and well known for its opening verse (Hosea 14:2), "Return O Israel to the Eternal your God."

We have seen, then, that the early centuries featured two reading cycles for Torah (annual and triennial), each with its own set of haftarot, and alternatives within each set. It has taken centuries to arrive at the order of haftarot we now have (there are still alternative traditions and options); centuries also to develop the exegetical traditions that define such staples as the "three haftarot of punishment," the "seven of consolation," and "the two of repentance." How and when did it all begin?

As with so much of Jewish liturgy, the haftarah's origins are uncertain. Contrary to popular imagination, it did not begin as a substitute for the banned reading of Torah in antiquity – as surmised by the fourteenth-century Spanish savant, David Abudarham. Nor does the haftarah go back all the way to Ezra, as reported by other medieval authorities (Rabbenu Tam and Isaiah of Trani, ca. twelfth–thirteenth centuries). An accurate reconstruction is often thought largely to depend on how we read two related reports in Luke/Acts. In Acts 13:15, Paul visits a synagogue on the Sabbath and delivers an address following "the reading of the law and the prophets." We are given no details. In Luke 4:16–19, Jesus himself attends and reads Isaiah 61:1–2, a prediction of his own anointing. If the point is the miracle by which he just happens to attend on the day that the required reading predicts his coming, we would already have a prescribed set of lections. More likely, however, Jesus is merely selecting an apt passage on his own.

More substantively, we should wonder whether these readings were indeed already part of a synagogue service of worship. The synagogue was not yet the rabbinic bastion that it eventually became, and the worship service that we now associate with it had not yet been established there. The first-century CE synagogue inscription by an otherwise unknown donor named Theodotus concurs with the New Testament evidence on the existence of scriptural readings in the synagogue, as do Josephus and even Philo from

Alexandria (also first century CE); but these readings need not have been connected to worship. The prophetic readings referred to in these early sources are not haftarot, therefore, so much as they are prophetic selections that served as the focus for study and debate, independent of worship.

Our current haftarah practice may be an evolution of this earlier practice. Alternatively, it emerged independently as part of rabbinic worship within rabbinic circles and moved into the synagogue when the rabbinic liturgy found its home there – a slow process, in all probability lasting from the second to the fourth century.

The theological purpose of the haftarah – the message of divine consolation and promise – can be seen from early midrashic collections that retain homilies based upon them. To this evidence should be added a talmudic citation of two prayers on which, it is said, we depend in times of travail: *k'dushah d'sidra* and *y'hei sh'mei rabba d'agad'ta*. The former (still recited in the morning service) is a pastiche of biblical verses that features "Holy, holy, holy" (*kadosh, kadosh, kadosh*) from Isaiah 6:3 – and is therefore called a *K'dushah*; this particular *K'dushah* begins with the promise "A redeemer will come to Zion." The latter cites the congregational response to the Kaddish, *y'hei sh'mei rabba* [*m'varakh*] ("May God's great name [be praised]"), but locates it as part of the *agad'ta* – the homily that it followed. Each Torah lection (called a *sidra*, in Palestine) ended on a promise of hope; the haftarah followed with a prophetic guarantee of Israel's future; the homily (the *agad'ta*) came next, underscoring better times to come; and the *Kaddish*, or *K'dushah d'sidra* = the *K'dushah* of the *sidra*, concluded the liturgical flow, with the guarantee that God's Kingdom would arrive and a redeemer would come to Zion.

It is no longer clear that the haftarot fulfill the same function today. Their connection to the Torah reading has largely been obscured by time; most people see them unrelated altogether – especially in synagogues where the Torah reading may not be recited in its entirety, so that the haftarah may relate to a part of the original reading that no one has even heard. Sermons are rarely related to the haftarah anymore. The two prayers that follow (*Kaddish* and *K'dushah d'sidra*) are slurred over in their original Hebrew and Aramaic without regard to what they mean, or omitted altogether because their significance has been forgotten. The very context and content of the haftarot are likely to be lost upon worshipers who hear them only in Hebrew – which they do not understand.

But Judaism revolves about the prophetic guarantee that God loves us, that the universe is not inimical to our interests, and that life can have meaning – for entire peoples and for individuals as well. The ultimate message of the haftarot – comfort, consolation, and hope – remains as relevant now as ever.

Introduction to *Nevi'im*

MARC ZVI BRETTLER

Duke University

INTRODUCTION

Nevi'im – literally "prophets," the second part of the Jewish biblical canon – is made up of of two parts: the Former Prophets and the Latter Prophets. The title "Prophets" is especially appropriate to the Latter Prophets, encompassing Isaiah, Jeremiah, Ezekiel, and the twelve Minor (in the sense of "short") Prophets, as these books contain what we would consider prophecy. The Former Prophets are not predominantly a record of the words of the God of Israel to Israel via intermediaries, but are rather an account of Israelite "history" beginning with the settlement of the land of Israel and ending soon after the Babylonian exile of 586 – from entrance into the land through exile from it. In that sense these books are often seen as more similar to history than prophecy. But they mention prophets such as Joshua, Nathan, Gad, Samuel, Elijah, and Elisha. As such, the Former Prophets naturally follow the Torah, which in its final book, Deuteronomy, promises that prophecy will continue after Moses's death: "The Lord your God will raise up for you a prophet from among your own people, like myself" (18:15; cf. v. 18).

THE FORMER PROPHETS

This section comprises four books: Joshua, Judges, Samuel, and Kings. Non-Jewish biblical manuscripts divide Samuel and Kings into four books: First Samuel, Second Samuel, First Kings and Second Kings. This division into four, already found in the Septuagint, the ancient translation of the Hebrew Bible into Greek, is secondary and problematic; for example, the division of Samuel puts the death of Saul both at the end of 1 Samuel and at the beginning of 2 Samuel, disrupting the narrative flow. Through the Middle Ages, Jews considered Samuel and Kings as single books. The halving of these books in the Greek, and then the Christian, and eventually the Jewish tradition was probably due to technical considerations – they are each too long to fit on the typical ancient scroll. Former Prophets is different from the second part of the Christian canon, Historical Works, which contains several more works – Ruth, Esther, Chronicles, Ezra, and Nehemiah – that are found in the final section of the Jewish canon, *Ketuvim* or Writings.

Joshua-Kings presents successive periods of the "history" of Israel: Joshua, from the death of Moses through the death of Joshua, and the conquest of much of the land of Israel; Judges, from the period that follows the main conquest until the rise of the monarchy; Samuel, from the rise of the monarchy as mediated by the prophet Samuel followed by the two first kings, Saul and David; and Kings – the successors of David – from Solomon through Zedekiah, the last king of Judah, concluding with a brief episode about the improvement of the lot of King Jehoiachin while imprisoned in Babylonia. Thus, these books also describe evolving types of leadership. Joshua is a prophetic military leader of all Israel, the judges are charismatic military leaders of smaller parts of Israel, and Samuel is a prophet who anoints kings – the main focus of the last two books.

At first glance, the Former Prophets offer a unified, sequential "history." Closer examination, however, indicates that this is not so – its books differ thematically and in style, emphasis, and vocabulary, and, in places, are out of chronological sequence (see e.g., Judg 17–21 and 2 Sam 21 and 24). They are thus each individual compositions, written and edited over a long time-period in an attempt to fill in the "history" of what happened between conquest and exile. It is quite possible that some of the books written to tell the earlier part of this "history" were composed, by and large, after those that narrate the later part of this period. For example, parts of Joshua and Judges were written in the exilic (586–538 BCE) period or even later, after the core of Kings was completed.

It is likely, however, that these four books were edited together to form a single whole; this explains certain thematic and vocabulary commonalities that are shared with the previous biblical book, the last book of the Torah, Deuteronomy. For this reason, from the middle of the twentieth century many biblical scholars have followed the position of the German Protestant biblical scholar Martin Noth, and have called Deuteronomy-Kings the Deuteronomic (or Deuteronomistic) History. More recently, some scholars have emphasized that the Former Prophets continue the story of the Pentateuch, and speak of the Bible's first nine books as a corpus, the Enneateuch ("nine books": Genesis, Exodus, Leviticus, Numbers, Deuteronomy, Joshua, Judges, Samuel, Kings). Though neither of these models is fully compelling, they each highlight the problems of considering Joshua, Judges, Samuel, and Kings as the only possible grouping worthy of consideration.

Yet, Joshua-Kings does present a logical assemblage of books, all focused on the land of Israel. Joshua narrates the conquest of the land; Joshua 21:41 notes: "The Lord gave to Israel the whole country which He had sworn to their fathers that He would assign to them; they took possession of it and settled in it." Judges, by and large, narrates attempts by foreign nations to conquer parts of the land and God helping Israel maintain that land through judges – charismatic military leaders. The enemies of the final judge, Samson, are the Philistines, who continue to plague Israel through Samuel, necessitating the more permanent institution of kingship, which continues, in different forms, throughout Samuel and Kings.

The Former Prophets is, however, much more than a narration of the time between conquest and exile. As part of the Bible it is primarily a theological work, which focuses on why the people of Israel merit possession of the land of Israel. As such, it is closely allied with a main theme of much of the Bible, especially Deuteronomy: *b'rit* or covenant. The biblical word *b'rit* means a "treaty," and, when used in the theologized sense of a covenant, it refers to the treaty between God and Israel, where Israel is rewarded for following God's norms by being given the possession of the land of Israel.

It is difficult for many readers in the diaspora to appreciate how central the possession of the land of Israel is to the Bible as a whole, and to the Former Prophets in particular, but this centrality is evident in each book in this corpus. For example, shortly before his death Joshua tells the people: "If you break the covenant that the Lord your God enjoined upon you, and go and serve other gods and bow down to them, then the Lord's anger will burn against you, and you shall quickly perish from the good land that He has given you" (Josh 23:16). In Judges 10:11-14, the Lord tells the nation: "[I have rescued you] from the Egyptians, from the Amorites, from the Ammonites, and from the Philistines.... and when you cried out to Me, I saved you from them. Yet you have forsaken Me and have served other gods. No, I will not deliver you again." Samuel threatens Israel, noting: "Thus said the Lord, the God of Israel: 'I brought Israel out of Egypt, and I delivered you from the hands of the Egyptians and of all the kingdoms that oppressed you.'" (1 Sam 10:18). Kings first tells of the exile of the Northern Kingdom, which was established, according to that book, after the death of Solomon. It was exiled to Assyria in approximately 722 "because the Israelites sinned against the Lord their God, who had freed them from the land of Egypt, from the hand of Pharaoh King of Egypt. They worshiped other gods" (2 Kings 17:7); as a result of this apostasy, "The Lord was incensed at Israel and He banished them from His presence" (2 Kings 17:18). Judah would be exiled a century and a half later, and one of the editors of the Book of Kings suggests that this was punishment for the sins of one of its later kings, Manasseh. 2 Kings 21:10-15, for example, narrates:

> Therefore the Lord spoke through His servants the prophets: "Because King Manasseh of Judah has done these abhorrent things – he has outdone in wickedness all that the Amorites did before his time – and because he led Judah to sin with his fetishes, assuredly, thus said the Lord, the God of Israel: I am going to bring such a disaster on Jerusalem and Judah that

both ears of everyone who hears about it will tingle.... I will wipe Jerusalem clean as one wipes a dish and turns it upside down. And I will cast off the remnant of My own people and deliver them into the hands of their enemies. They shall be plunder and prey to all their enemies because they have done what is displeasing to Me and have been vexing Me from the day that their fathers came out of Egypt to this day."

Together, these passages, to which many more could be added, highlight the nature of the Former Prophets as a theological composition, emphasizing that only through covenant obedience is Israel protected from its enemies and rewarded with land. Within the ancient Near Eastern world in which the Bible was written, gods are typically imagined to be involved in their nations' history, punishing and rewarding them appropriately. Yet none of these non-Israelite accounts emphasizes covenant in the same manner or to the same extent.

Earlier in this essay, I several times used the word "history" with quotation marks around it. We now use that word in many different senses, referring to both events that transpired, and accounts that narrate such events. Clearly, the Latter Prophets are history in that second sense. In modern times, we consider the accuracy of the historical account to be of paramount importance, but that was not the case in antiquity. Thus, the Bible in general, and the Former Prophets in particular, are history in the sense that they are a narrative of a past, but not in the sense of a(n accurate) narrative of the past. Stated differently, some parts of the Former Prophets may be used to reconstruct what actually happened in ancient Israel, but much of it may not.

Four reasons suggest to scholars that these books should not be read as straightforward history. First, interest in objective history-writing did not exist in the ancient world, and has only been a scholarly ideal for a century and a half. Second, linguistic evidence suggests that many of the accounts now found in the Latter Prophets were written centuries after the events that they purport to narrate, and such accounts are extremely malleable over time.

Third, the Latter Prophets are full of competing narratives concerning historical events. For example, Joshua is inconsistent about whether or not the entire land was conquered (compare, e.g., 21:43 with 13:2–6); Samuel in one place attributes the death of Goliath the giant to David (1 Sam 17), but elsewhere to Elḥanan (2 Sam 21:19); the siege of Jerusalem by Sennacherib in 701 is depicted through at least three differing intertwined accounts in 2 Kings 18–19. (The presence of multiple and even contradictory accounts within a single biblical book permeates the Bible, which is a collection of collections, and is one fundamental way that the Bible as a book differs from contemporary books that we typically encounter.) Fourth, in some cases the historical record as known from non-biblical sources disproves the biblical account. This is most evident in Joshua, where the archeological record contradicts that book's predominant account of a swift and complete Israelite conquest of the land. This contradiction is so sharp that most biblical historians speak of the settlement of the land rather than its conquest. Archaeology similarly suggests that the extensive United Monarchy, founded, according to Samuel-Kings by David, did not exist. Some contemporary biblical scholars point to the Tel Dan inscription excavated in 1993–1994, which mentions "the house of David," to suggest that David himself did exist, while others note that this inscription is at least a century later than when King David would have lived, and thus has no bearing on the historical David. These insights about lack of historicity are not meant to denigrate the Bible; they are not value judgments, but are meant to show that the Latter Prophets may not be used as straightforward historical accounts.

Instead, this large corpus should be read as a highly theologized portrayal of the period between settlement and exile. In some cases, real events are recast in a theological mold, while other events may reflect the creative shaping of the past to illustrate particular theological or ideological concerns. Thus, readers of these books should concentrate more on what the text is trying to say, especially about Israel's relationship to its God, rather than on whether the narrative comports with what we know from extra-biblical sources.

THE LATTER PROPHETS

The books of the Latter Prophets – Isaiah, Jeremiah, Ezekiel, and the Minor Prophets (also called The Twelve) – all purport to contain prophecies, namely, words revealed by God to prophets, individuals specially chosen to convey the divine word. Contrary to the common belief, the main function of prophecy was not predicting the future, but warning Israel (and in some cases other nations) about proper behavior, and explaining why Israel has been punished. The latter function of prophecy is typically under-appreciated by modern readers, but is especially evident, for example, in much of Isaiah 1–39, which, instead of calling on Israel to repent, emphasizes that it is being punished for abandoning its God and relying instead on the political power of the Assyrians to save it. The de-emphasis of repentance is most striking in that prophet's inaugural vision, where he states in the name of God: "Dull that people's mind, Stop its ears, And seal its eyes – Lest, seeing with its eyes and hearing with its ears, it also grasp with its mind, and repent and save itself" (6:10).

A canonical section on prophecy appears as the final section of the Christian Old Testament. It differs in two ways from the comparable section in the Hebrew Bible. It is larger, containing the Book of Daniel, which is found in *Ketuvim*, Writings, in the Hebrew Bible. Also, in the Christian canon, Prophets are the final part of the Old Testament, leading directly into the Gospels about Jesus, whose arrival they are understood to predict; in the Jewish *Tanakh*, the Major Prophets are at the physical center of the Hebrew Bible, and understood as subordinate to the initial Torah.

The belief that deities communicated with their people was common in the ancient Near Eastern world. Such deities were believed to commune in a variety of ways, including through omens. Although a small number of prophecies like those found in the Latter Prophets are found in the ancient Near Eastern world, these are relatively few in number and have not been collected together to form anything similar to the prophetic books that make up the Latter Prophets. Exactly why this form developed specifically in ancient Israel has not been satisfactorily explained.

The prophets included in the Latter Prophets cover a wide time period and geographical distribution. (It is likely that other such prophetic collections existed in ancient Israel, but have not been preserved.) The earliest are Hosea and Amos, from the eighth-century Northern Kingdom; the latest are from the post-exilic period, from the late sixth century and after. Most prophesied in Judah, but others in northern Israel, Babylonia, Persia, and Egypt. Given this broad chronological and geographical distribution, it should not be surprising that these books are quite diverse in theme, structure, and style.

Yet, several themes tie together many of these prophets. These include the idea that, even though Israel's God is the God of all people and holds them all accountable for grave moral failings, God has a special relationship with Israel, whom he rewards for proper behavior and punishes for covenant infractions. While some prophets emphasize ethical breaches and others highlight religious or cultic infractions, both of these elements are viewed as part of the covenant. The Israelite prophets sometimes inveigh against Israelites who are punctilious in their performance of rituals while they oppress the underclasses, but, contrary to what is frequently said, this is only a small part of the prophetic message. Although different prophetic books contain different mixtures of encouragement, consolation, and gloom and doom, taken as a whole the prophetic material is ultimately optimistic, looking forward to the arrival of a "Day of the Lord," when God's power will be especially evident and the wicked will be punished.

Individuals called prophets also appear in the books that precede the Latter Prophets. Abraham is called a prophet (Gen 20:7), and Moses, the protagonist of much of the Torah, is depicted as the greatest prophet ever (Deut 34:10). The Former Prophets describe a wide variety of named and unnamed prophets; this provides some continuity between the two parts of the canonical section *Nevi'im.* Yet, the prophets described in the Former Prophets are quite different from those depicted in the Latter prophets. The former speak, but briefly, and typically in prose, often focus on the king, and perform miracles. The latter, frequently called by scholars "classical prophets," often speak at length and in poetry, to the population as a whole, and perform non-miraculous symbolic actions. The title *ish-elohim*, "man of God," typifies some of the former, while *navi* (plural *nevi'im*), "prophet," which likely means "one who was called," typifies the latter.

The appearance of the section *Nevi'im* immediately following the Torah may suggest that the prophets should be understood as calling upon the people of Israel to observe the Torah, and this is indeed how classical Jewish sources understand this section. Modern critical biblical scholarship, however, has shown that the Torah came into being over a long period of time, as did the prophetic corpus, so that the Torah and the prophetic corpus developed side by side; thus the latter should not be seen as an interpretation of the former. This explains why the Torah is cited or quoted so infrequently in the Prophets, and why passages in the Prophets may disagree with the Torah.

Many of the introductions to the Latter Prophets contain superscriptions that place the words of the prophets in a particular historical setting, such as Isaiah 1:1: "The prophecies of Isaiah son of Amoz, who prophesied concerning Judah and Jerusalem in the reigns of Uzziah, Jotham, Ahaz, and Hezekiah, kings of Judah." This highlights something important about most biblical prophecy – it is not vague and general, but specifically oriented to particular events during the prophet's lifetime. It is thus useful to read prophetic books alongside a history of Israel, which outlines these events.

But, as modern scholarship has shown, it is unlikely that all of the words found in a prophetic book were recited by the prophet to whom they are attributed. The prophets themselves did not write the books that are called by their names – this was likely done later, likely by their students and other individuals, and was a process that transpired over several generations; these works were written in an era that lacked the idea of copyright. For example, one of the editors of Jeremiah was closely affiliated with the school influenced by Deuteronomy, and added whole oracles to that book in the flavor of Deuteronomy – in Jeremiah's name. Also, the Book of Isaiah has been supplemented several times, and contains works of several prophets, and a new ending was added to Amos, making it more optimistic. Such additions to works in the name of their original authors typify ancient writing, and may reflect the reverential attitude of the editor toward the original author, whom he wanted to augment and "clarify." In some cases, editors of prophetic books copied from one another, or from common oral or written sources, as suggested by the nearly identical words describing an idyllic future in Isaiah 2 and Micah 4. Scholars often debate precisely which parts are original to a prophetic book and which are not, but all agree that it is important to differentiate between the words of the prophet and the content of the prophetic book.

In this brief introduction, it is possible only to begin to introduce each prophetic book. Isaiah is the most poetic of the Latter Prophets, and the book contains material ranging from the eighth century though the exilic period (chaps. 40–55 – often called Deutero-Isaiah), and likely beyond (chaps. 56–66 – often called Trito-Isaiah). Jeremiah lived before and after the destruction of the First Temple in 586; much of the book focuses on this event. Ezekiel, a priest, was exiled to Babylonia in 597, and he experienced the destruction of 586 long-distance – this helps to explain much of his prophecy.

The Minor Prophets, as its other name, "The Twelve," suggests, is a collection of twelve different short prophetic books. The same books appear together in the Hebrew and Greek Bibles, though they are ordered differently in each. The standard Hebrew order, now found in Jewish Bibles, is: Hosea, Joel, Amos, Obadiah, Jonah, Micah, Nahum, Habakkuk, Zephaniah, Haggai, Zechariah, and Malakhi. These twelve short books range in size from one (Obadiah) to fourteen chapters (Zechariah), and many of them are composite collections. They were likely copied together onto one scroll, to create a single book, because small books, on small pieces of parchment, were in danger of getting lost. These are ordered in what was imagined to be chronological order, with the earliest from eighth-century northern Israel (Hosea, Amos), and the latest from post-exilic Judah/Yehud (Haggai, Zechariah, Malakhi), thus covering prophesies from a period of at least three centuries. Most are similar in content to the longer Major Prophets. Jonah, the best-known minor prophet, is exceptional; it is mostly about the prophet rather than concerned with preserving what he said, and Jonah is sent to a foreign nation rather than to Israel. As an outlier, it highlights the diversity found within the Latter Prophets.

Many of the prophetic oracles are in poetry. Biblical poetry, like modern poetry, contains metaphors, similes, and word-plays, but it differs from much Western poetry in many ways. For one, it is not typified by rhyme or rhythm. Instead, most biblical poetic lines are binary, and the second half often restates or extends the first half, or expresses the same idea in an opposite fashion – a form called parallelism. The following layout of Amos 1:2 makes this structure evident:

> The Lord roars from Zion,
>> Shouts aloud from Jerusalem;
> And the pastures of the shepherds shall languish,
>> And the summit of Carmel shall wither.

Much, but not all, of biblical prophecy is preserved in such parallelistic poetry, which highlights the divine word as having special power.

THE PROPHETS IN JUDAISM

The *Nevi'im* play an important role in later Jewish tradition, but one that is distinctly subsidiary to the Torah. Unlike the Torah, which is read as a whole as part of the lectionary, only sections of the prophets are read as part of the haftarah, the prophetic reading cycle. Certain parts of the *Nevi'im* were also highlighted by the significant liturgical role that they gained, such as Isaiah 6:3, "Holy, holy, holy! The Lord of Hosts! His presence fills all the earth!," which is at the core of the *Kedusha* or sanctification prayer. Other biblical prayers cite or rework sections of the Prophets. For example, the section in the prayer in the weekday Amidah (lit. "standing"), the thrice daily statutory prayer, concerning the restoration of the Davidic monarchy, begins "may you make flourish the branch of David";

this is based on Zechariah 3:8, which refers to the Davidic king as "My servant the Branch." The conclusion of the Aleinu prayer, which ends the evening, morning, and afternoon services, quotes Zechariah 14:9: "And the Lord shall be king over all the earth; in that day there shall be one Lord with one name." Thus, through the liturgy, the average Jew would have been familiar with parts of this corpus, but not its entirety. And in general, the Latter Prophets rather than the Former Prophets played a more important role in post-biblical Judaism, though certain figures from the Former Prophets, such as David and Elijah, remain very significant.

Judaism reinterpreted the Latter Prophets in a fundamental way – understanding the prophets not as addressing (only) their generation, but as speaking to later generations of Jews. This is visible already in the Dead Sea Scrolls, from the late Second Temple period, where a genre called Pesher Literature interprets texts from Isaiah, Nahum, Habakkuk, and other works as referring to events transpiring centuries later. The same tendency undergirds the New Testament, especially Matthew, where older prophecies are seen as fulfilled with Jesus in the first century of the common era; here it is important to recall that most of the earliest Christians were Jewish. The classical rabbis and most classical medieval interpreters also understood the Latter Prophets not as arcane speakers only to their contemporaries, but as voicing universal, ever-relevant truths.

The *Nevi'im* also had some limited impact on later Jewish law. For example, the rabbinic prohibition against carrying on Shabbat is related to Jeremiah 17:21, "Guard yourselves for your own sake against carrying burdens on the Sabbath day." But the greatest impact of the *Nevi'im* remains the hopeful prophecies it offers for an ideal, messianic future, such as expressed in Isaiah 2:4, "And they shall beat their swords into plowshares and their spears into pruning hooks: Nation shall not take up sword against nation; they shall never again know war," which not only reflects a Jewish ideal, but is etched in stone outside the United Nations.

Introduction to *Ketuvim*

DEBORAH KAHN-HARRIS

Leo Baeck College

KETUVIM IS IS THE THIRD AND FINAL SECTION OF THE HEBREW
Bible, or *Tanakh*. Known in English as "Writings" (the literal translation of the Hebrew word *Ketuvim*), it is also known by its Greek
title, Hagiographa. Though scholars are by no means in agreement
about the origins of the tripartite division of the Hebrew Bible, one
possible explanation for the source of *Ketuvim* is that it stems from
the addition of the Book of Psalms – the first book of *Ketuvim* – as
a third section following the already existing division between Law
(Torah) and Prophecy (*Nevi'im*). Indeed, as the current order of the
Hebrew Bible stands, the Book of Psalms, as the first work in *Ketuvim*, functions as a kind of border between *Nevi'im* and *Ketuvim*, a
boundary not only in virtue of its position, but also as it straddles
the difference between books with consistent and frequent liturgical usage and those with less common usage, as well as between
books with fairly stable and fixed texts and those with texts that
remained more fluid to a later date. *Ketuvim* as a unified work may
date to the last centuries before the Common Era, but may equally
date much later, into the early rabbinic period, perhaps around the
second century CE.

Whatever the dating of the final recension of *Ketuvim*, what is
clear is that it is not a single, unified work at all. In effect, *Ketuvim*
is the miscellaneous file of the Hebrew Bible, the all-too-often
unexplored treasure trove at the end of the *Tanakh*. Each of the
eleven books of *Ketuvim* – from different time periods, with different

authorship issues, different genres, different lengths, and much more to differentiate them besides – could have a lengthy introduction of its own. And each work in *Ketuvim* is unique; every one is a precious jewel to be savored and studied. Indeed, so exciting are these works in their own rights that it's very challenging to limit each to a brief introduction.

Ketuvim consists of the following works:

1. Psalms/*Tehillim*
2. Proverbs/*Mishlei*
3. Job/*Iyov*
4. The Song of Songs /*Shir HaShirim*
5. Ruth/*Rut*
6. Lamentations/*Eikha*
7. Ecclesiastes/*Kohelet*
8. Esther/*Ester*
9. Daniel/*Daniel*
10. Ezra/*Ezra* – Nehemiah/*Nehemiah*
11. 1 *&* 2 Chronicles/ *Divrei HaYamim*

This order, as it currently appears in a Hebrew Bible, is a comparatively modern arrangement. The order appears to be based on a loose thematic grouping of the texts into *Sifre Emet, Hameish Megillot,* and the remaining books. *Sifre Emet* is an acronym drawn from the Hebrew names of first three books – *aleph* (Job), *mem* (Proverbs), *tav* (Psalms) spelling out *emet,* truth; hence, "the books of truth." Job and Proverbs (as well as potentially some individual Psalms) are formally classified as wisdom literature, which may also help explain why they have been grouped together. *Hameish Megillot* are the five shorter scrolls which are read as part of Jewish festival observance. The Megillot appear here in festival order beginning with Song of Songs, which is read (at least in Ashkenazi communities) on the intermediate Shabbat of Pesah; Ruth, which is read on Shavuot; Lamentations, which is read on Tisha B'Av; Ecclesiastes, which is read on the intermediate Shabbat of Sukkot in Ashkenazi communities and on Shemini Atzeret in some Sephardi and other communities (as per Rashi); and Esther, which is read on Purim. The final section, therefore, is made up of the books that remain – Daniel, Ezra-Nehemiah, and Chronicles. All of these works are late, which likely accounts for their placement at the end of the Hebrew Bible. In addition, the note of substantial hope which concludes Chronicles – the proclamation of Cyrus to allow the Jews to return to Jerusalem and rebuild the Temple – perhaps accounts for Chronicles' placement as the final book of the Hebrew Bible.

In the Babylonian Talmud Bava Batra 14b–15a, on the other hand, we find a different discussion of the order and authorship of both *Nevi'im* and *Ketuvim*. The order of *Ketuvim* given there is as follows: Ruth, Psalms, Job, Proverbs, Ecclesiastes, Song of Songs, Lamentations, Daniel, Esther, Ezra (which included Nehemiah), and Chronicles (as a single work). This order is chronological, based on ascription of authorship as follows: Moses wrote Job; Samuel wrote Ruth; David wrote Psalms along with the help of ten elders; Jeremiah wrote Lamentations; Proverbs, Songs of Songs, and Ecclesiastes are ascribed to Hezekiah; the Men of the Great Assembly[1] wrote Daniel and Esther; and Ezra (with Nehemiah writing the concluding section) wrote Ezra and Chronicles. Two notable problems arise, though, from this list. The first, as acknowledged in the Talmud, is that Job, according to this reckoning, is the oldest book in *Ketuvim*. The explanation given for this is that Job begins with calamity, which the rabbis deemed not appropriate for beginning a section of the Hebrew Bible; Job, therefore, must predate this custom. Ruth, the Talmud counters, also begins with calamity, but calamity which has a good end, i.e., the birth of the child who is the ancestor of King David. The second problem is that the Bava Batra passage ascribes Proverbs, Song of Songs, and Ecclesiastes to Hezekiah. These works, however, were all widely understood to have been written by Solomon, which would have placed them chronologically before Jeremiah's Lamentations. The ascription here is instead understood to mean that Hezekiah and his men

---

1 Traditionally, an assembly of 120 rabbis that ruled for approximately two centuries, from the period after the time of the prophets up until 70 CE.

copied and/or published these works, rather than wrote them. Presumably the origin of this idea lies in Proverbs 25:1, "These are also the proverbs of Solomon which the men of King Hezekiah of Judah transcribed." Assigning these works to Hezekiah serves as an explanation for why Lamentations should precede them.

For the purposes of the remainder of this introduction the current standard order of *Ketuvim* will be used.

PSALMS

The title of this book, Psalms, comes from the Septuagint and means an "ode," or words set to music. The Hebrew title, *Tehillim*, simply means praises. The Book of Psalms includes one hundred and fifty separate psalms, which are largely short poetic works. Psalm 119, at 176 verses, is the longest of the Psalms, but most are far shorter. The Psalter itself is subdivided into five sections (Psalms 1-41; 42-72; 73-89; 90-106; 107-150), likely in imitation of the Pentateuch. Beyond this division, a number of distinct collections appear in the Psalms, including, for example, the Hallel psalms, Psalms 113-118, and the so-called Psalms of Ascent, Psalms 120-134. Dating and authorship vary from psalm to psalm, with some individual psalms believed to be very ancient indeed. The final redaction of the Psalter into its current form is widely agreed to be post-exilic, probably dating to the Second Temple period. Throughout the twentieth century the main approach to classifying the psalms has been Gunkel's form criticism, which organizes them into the following genres (with smaller subcategories in a number of these areas): Individual complaints, Communal complaints, Individual Psalms of thanksgiving, Royal Psalms, Psalms of Enthronement, and Hymns.

The psalms are likely to have their origins in liturgical usage, with many psalms still in use this way today in Jewish practice. For example, in addition to the recitation of Hallel on festivals, Psalm 27 is added to daily prayer during the month of Elul. Psalms 29 and 95-99 are read on Friday evenings (a practice introduced by the Kabbalists), and the daily morning service contains a psalm for each day of the week, beginning with Sunday: Psalms 24, 48, 82, 94, and part of 95, 81, and 93. Psalm 145, prefaced by Psalm 84:5 and 144:15, and Psalm 150 form part of the weekday morning service's *pesuqei d'zimra* section, and Psalm 24 or 29 is sung during the procession at the end of the Torah service as the scroll is returned to the ark. Several psalms, including, famously, Psalm 23, are often recited at funerals and in a house of mourning. Psalms are also traditionally recited at the bedside of a person who is ill.

PROVERBS

The Book of Proverbs is really a compilation of several shorter works of wisdom literature. Traditionally, as has been noted, Proverbs is ascribed to King Solomon, particularly because of the superscription at the beginning of the work: "The proverbs of Solomon son of David, King of Israel." Dating issues abound, with no academic consensus. Various arguments have been put forward, with dates ranging from 900–200 BCE.

The sections of Proverbs are not in dispute, as the book is clearly laid out. Of the eight sections, only the final section does not have a title demarcated by the text itself. The component parts of Proverbs with their various appellations are as follows:

1. Proverbs 1–9: "The proverbs of Solomon, the son of David, King of Israel"
2. Proverbs 10:1–22:16: "The proverbs of Solomon"
3. Proverbs 22:17–24:22 (the title here is embedded in the Masoretic Text): "The words of the wise"
4. Proverbs 24:23–34: "These are also by the wise"
5. Proverbs 25:1–29:27: "These are also the proverbs of Solomon which the men of King Hezekiah of Judah transcribed"
6. Proverbs 30:1–33: "The words of Agur son of Yakeh the Massaite," etc.
7. Proverbs 31:1–9: "The words of Lemuel King of Massa with which his mother admonished him"

8. Proverbs 31:10–31: no formal title, however an alphabetic acrostic poem[2]

These collections are, overall, very different from one another. For example, Proverbs 1–9 is structured as instructions to a son, with particular reference to the figure of "Lady Wisdom" and an admonition against folly. Proverbs 10:1–22:16, by contrast, is simply a collection of sayings, which many scholars have compared to the Egyptian wisdom work *The Instruction of Amenemope*. While the structure of different sections may be distinct, as a whole Proverbs relies heavily on the use of both antithetic (the juxtaposition of opposing ideas, e.g., Prov 11:1) and synonymous (the repetition of ideas through the use of similar terminology, e.g., Prov 9:10) parallelism to create meaning.

The Book of Proverbs as a whole is not recited in Jewish liturgy, but certain individual sections are. The final poem, Proverbs 31:10–31, for example, is well known as *eishet ḥayil*, "the woman of valor," a title taken from this poem's first line, and is traditionally recited by a husband to his wife as part of the home ceremonies on erev Shabbat. Proverbs 4:2, followed by 3:18 and then 3:17, form part of the liturgy for the end of the Torah service recited as the scroll is returned to the ark. Proverbs 3:18, in particular ("It [wisdom/Torah] is a tree of life for all who take hold of it…") has become one of the most recognisable verses in the Torah because of the many popular melodies that have been composed for it.

JOB

The Book of Job, the second of the three books of wisdom literature in *Ketuvim*, is perhaps best described as a theodicy, or at least as some sort of existential response to the problem of evil in the universe. Authorship, aside from the talmudic designation, is unknown.

---

2   An acrostic is a poem or other composition in which the first letters of each line spell out another word, or correspond to the letters of the alphabet in the correct order; hence, Lam 1:1 begins with א, Lam 1:2 ב, Lam 1:3 ג, and so on.

Dating, too, is unclear, though a date between the sixth–fourth centuries BCE is generally advanced.

The structure of Job is two-fold. First is the framing story found in Job 1–2 and 42:7–17. Here, the narrative portion of the book is laid out: Job is a blameless man who fears God. But, when God mentions Job's behavior to the Adversary (Satan), Satan suggests that Job is only moral because his life is comfortable; hence, Job is afflicted to see whether he will curse God or remain upright. Once afflicted, Job's three friends, Eliphaz the Temanite, Bildad the Shuhite, and Zophar the Naamathite, come to console him. The second section of Job is found in Job 3:1 through 42:6, which forms the bulk of the book. This section includes a series of dialogues, first in Job 3–31 between Job and his three friends, then in Job 32–37 with the words of a fourth (previously unmentioned) friend, Elihu the Buzite, and finally in Job 38–41:16 with the dialogues between God and Job. The final section of the book is the remainder of the narrative frame, the divine speeches wherein God chastises Job's friends and restores Job's good fortune.

Theologically, the Book of Job has been both compelling and challenging to traditional exegetes and contemporary academics alike. When God answers Job out of the whirlwind in Job 38:1, God does not truly explain to Job why he must suffer; the two responses God makes to Job contain no real answers. First, God essentially overwhelms Job with questions: Who are you to speak with me? Where were you when I created the world? Have you ever had my degree of responsibility? What do you really know? What can you actually do? Who are you to complain? Job's brief response in Job 40:3–5 merely elicits a second, even less satisfactory, reply from God, as God describes the creation of the fantastical creatures, the behemoth and the leviathan. Job is left in Job 42:1–6 simply acknowledging that God is omnipotent and that he, Job, spoke without understanding; thus, being only dust and ashes, he racants.

The theological challenge of the Book of Job is still relevant today. While not used liturgically, the question of God's presence when people suffer is, of course, no less a question for people today than it was for the determinedly non-Israelite Job and his friends.

SONG OF SONGS

The Song of Songs – perhaps better translated as "The Superlative Song" – is traditionally ascribed to the young King Solomon. The Song of Songs is an extended love poem (or poems) in three voices – a female lover, a male lover, and a feminine choral voice (the daughters of Jerusalem). Opinions vary as to whether the Song should be read as a unified whole or as a series of individual poems edited to become one, with no consensus about the potential demarcations between individual poems.

While no formal narrative as such exists in the Song of Songs, the Song does appear to have some type of framework, with a flow from beginning to end. The Song begins with the female lover addressing her male consort, imploring him to kiss her. She describes herself as "dark and comely" (1:5), while her male lover describes her in far more explicit terms in three separate sections of the Song (4:1–7; 6:4–7; 7:2–10). She describes his beauty as well (5:10–16). These descriptions are often likened, stylistically, to the later Arabic poetic form of the *wasf*. But, unlike the *wasf* and its focus on beauty, the Song of Songs is not all light and passion. Dark moments occur as well. In one passage, drunk with desire, the female lover wanders the night streets in search of her lover. She is discovered by the city guards and beaten, so begs the daughters of Jerusalem to find her lover for her (5:6–8). Perhaps the most pressing question that arises in the Song is whether the lovers ever consummate their relationship. The text is vague, but the almost obsessive nature of the lover's declarations to each other leave the reader in little doubt as to their intentions should they ever have the chance.

The opening superscription, "the song of songs that is Solomon's," is ambiguous; it is unclear whether the Song of Songs is authored by Solomon or dedicated to him. This ambiguity, alongside the prominent female voice within the Song, has led to suggestions of female authorship, proposing one of Solomon's lovers as author of the work. However, dating is much contested, with dates between the tenth to the second century BCE being posited, and the current consensus is largely for a later date, well after the time of Solomon.

While the most straightforward reading of the Song of Songs treats the Song as exquisite love poetry, in traditional Jewish exegesis the Song has long been interpreted as an allegory of God's relationship with the people of Israel. The Song of Songs is one of three books, the other two of which are Esther and Ecclesiastes, whose status is debated in the Mishnah and other classical sources, potentially because the Tetragrammaton appears nowhere in these books. Indeed, no straightforward reading of the Song of Songs reveals any name of God in the text. Notwithstanding, Rabbi Akiva (m. Yadayim 3:5) declares "the whole world is not as worthy as the day on which the Song of Songs was given to Israel."

In addition to its festival reading, the Song of Songs is read in some Hasidic circles on erev Shabbat. The reading of the Song at Pesaḥ is explained through the Song's allegorical interpretation, with both the liberation of the Israelites from Egypt and the Song of Songs understood as testaments to God's love for Israel. Modern renditions of particular verses, especially Nira Chen's song, "Dodi Li," based on Song of Songs 2:16; 3:6; 4:9 and 16, have become popular at weddings, perhaps echoing theories that the Song of Songs has its origins in ancient wedding celebrations.

RUTH

The Book of Ruth is a short novella, perhaps a romance as well, set during the time of the Judges – which explains its location in the Christian Old Testament following the Book of Judges. Ruth is a short work, a mere four chapters, with a tightly knit plot. The book is named after its eponymous heroine, Ruth, which directs the reader towards Ruth's function in the story. In fact, the book might just as easily have been named Naomi, as her role is arguably almost as large and central to the narrative as that of Ruth herself.

The plot is relatively uncomplicated. Naomi, her husband, and two sons migrate to the land of Moab following a famine in their hometown of Bethlehem. In Moab the sons marry local women,

Ruth and Orpah, but both the sons and Naomi's husband soon die. Naomi decides to return to Bethlehem, adjuring Ruth and Orpah to return to their familial homes. Orpah does so, but Ruth, in one of the most famous addresses in all of the Hebrew Bible, pleads to remain (1:16–17). Upon Ruth and Naomi's return to Bethlehem, in an effort to find food Ruth goes reaping in the fields of Boaz, a close kinsman of Naomi's. He acts kindly towards Ruth, and eventually Naomi contrives a plan for Ruth to persuade Boaz to marry her. After a scene on the threshing room floor and some legal wranglings around levirate marriage, Boaz and Ruth are married. Ruth becomes pregnant and the women of Bethlehem declare (4:17) that "a son is born to Naomi!" The book concludes with a genealogy from Perez (son of Judah and Tamar [Gen 38]) through to Obed, son of Boaz and Ruth/Naomi, finally ending two generations later with King David.

The plot of the story, ending with the genealogy of King David, has led to a date during the Monarchical period. Equally, some scholars believe that the plot – a non-Israelite, Moabite woman marrying an Israelite (forbidden by biblical law) and becoming the great-grandmother of King David – points to a date around the time of Ezra-Nehemiah when the narrative would have functioned as a polemic against the casting out of foreign wives.

As to why the story is read at Shavuot, explanations include:

1. The threshing-room floor scene is set during the barley harvest, the time of Shavuot.
2. Ruth chooses to stay with Naomi and accept the Israelite God, just as the children of Israel choose God at the revelation at Mt. Sinai, which is the historical basis for the festival of Shavuot.
3. Finally, according to legend, King David died on Shavuot.

LAMENTATIONS

The title, Lamentations, is a translation of the names of the work in both Greek, "Threnoi," and Rabbinic Hebrew, "Kinot." The Hebrew name currently in use is Eicha, after the first word of Lamentations

1:1, meaning "alas."[3] The work is composed of five chapters, each an individual poem, the first four of which are alphabetic acrostics (Lamentations 3 is a triple acrostic). As an extremely graphic, first-hand account of the fall of Jerusalem and subsequent destruction of the First Temple by the Babylonians, the book is generally dated to between 586–550 BCE.

The poems are largely voiced in the first person, with Zion personified as a woman the main speaking voice in Lamentations 1 and 2, "the man who has known affliction" the voice in Lamentations 3, and a different man, sometimes thought of as a reporter, the voice of Lamentations 4 . Lamentations 5 is a communal lament in the first person plural. While traditionally ascribed to Jeremiah (the Vulgate even adds the superscription "The Lamentations of Jeremiah"), current theories suggest that the work may have originated in a school of prophets or the Temple singers.[4]

Theologically, Lamentations is challenging. It can be bleak, portraying little, if any, hope. Although Lamentations 3 and 5 make some reference to the need for the people to return to God, Lamentations 1 and 2, in particular (but also parts of all of the other chapters), accuse God of deserting the people and having disproportionate anger towards them. Lamentations 1 and 2 also contain disturbing images of sexual violence and the cannibalism of children (which is repeated in Lamentations 4).

As a highly emotive and evocative description of the events of 587/586 BCE, Lamentations is traditionally read on Tisha B'Av, the fast day that commemorates the destruction of both Temples as well as numerous other catastrophes in Jewish history. Indeed, public reading of the scroll dates back to antiquity, perhaps even to the years immediately following the destruction of the Temple and the exile to Babylon. Lamentations 5:21 ("*Hashiveinu Adonai…*") is well

---

3 Eicha is also the first word of Lamentations 2:1 and 4:1.

4 A number of references to groups/schools of prophets appear in the Hebrew Bible (e.g., 1 Sam 10:5 & 19:20; 2 Kings 2:3 & 9:1). Who exactly these groups of prophets were and how they functioned is a subject of scholarly debate. The Temple Singers were a subsection of the Levites, who were assigned the duty of playing music and singing in the Temple. See 1 Chr 25:1–7.

known from its liturgical use both at the end of the Torah service, when the ark is closed following the return of the Torah scroll, and as part of the High Holiday liturgy in the *Shema Koleinu* prayer.

ECCLESIASTES

The third of the three books of wisdom literature in *Ketuvim*, Ecclesiastes presents the reader with yet another view of the genre. Apparently the work of a single author, Ecclesiastes is far shorter – at just twelve chapters – than either Proverbs or Job. The title of the work comes from the Greek translation of the Hebrew "*kohelet*," part of the superscription to this work: "These are the words of Kohelet, the son of David, king in Jerusalem." Kohelet means a "convenor," sometimes understood as a person who gathered others around in order to teach or instruct them; hence, "The Preacher." Traditionally, this preacher is understood to be Solomon, here reflecting on life from a position of advanced age.

The dating of Ecclesiastes is contested. Arguments based on linguistic and thematic issues suggest the late Persian period, around 450–330 BCE. On the basis of influence from Greek philosophy, particularly Stoicism and Epicureanism, others recommend a later date, between 330–180 BCE. Certainly Ecclesiastes is not later than 180 BCE, as it is quoted by Ben Sira.

The text itself is somewhat circular, arguing from different angles about both the meaning and meaningless of life. Numerous famous phrases appear repeatedly in the text: "There is nothing new under the sun," "Vanity of vanities, all is vanity," "Chasing after the wind," etc. Perhaps most famous of all is the poem that begins Ecclesiastes 3, which suggests that a time exists for everything in its turn. Yet, even this sentiment is upended by the book's repeated assertion of the futility of existence, triggering comparisons of Ecclesiastes to the works of Albert Camus and other existentialist philosophers.

Unlike Song of Songs, Ecclesiastes does mention God, but the Tetragrammaton does not appear in the text. Perhaps a concern with the theology of the text, therefore, is the reason for the addi-

tions beginning in Ecclesiastes 12:9, which are widely assumed to
have been added at a later point. Ecclesiastes 12:9 and 12 both begin,
"And he added"; also, fear of God and the observance of commandments is put forth in Ecclesiastes 9:13 as the proper conclusion to
The Preacher's musings – a conclusion much in opposition to the
bulk of the work.

As to why Ecclesiastes is read on Sukkot and/or Shemini Atzeret,
most explanations seem at best forced. The tradition is mentioned
by Rashi, so clearly goes back at least as far as the eleventh century,
if not earlier. Perhaps the reference to "eights" in Ecclesiastes 11:2,
which is understood by Kohelet Rabbah 11:2 as an allusion to Sukkot, is the best explanation for this tradition.Nonetheless, for many
people, Kohelet's reflective tone is reminiscent of the autumnal
season, homiletically (though not in any scholarly sense) linking
the book with Sukkot, the Autumn harvest festival.

ESTHER

The Book of Esther appears to be many things: a work of historical fiction, a romance, a comedy, the origin of the Jewish festival
of Purim, a blueprint for Jewish life in the diaspora, and more. A
fictional account set in the Persian court, the Book of Esther is
named after the work's heroine. Consensus is that Esther is late,
likely dating from the fourth century BCE.

The recension history of the Book of Esther is complex, with
six significant additions to the story appearing in the Septuagint.
But the plot of the Masoretic version of Esther is well known: a
beautiful young Jew, Esther (Hebrew name, Hadassah), marries King
Ahasuerus of Persia and hence is able to save her people from the
clutches of the evil Haman. Yet, the story is more complex than this
single line suggests. The book is also the story of Esther's foster-
father, Mordechai, a Benjaminite, as he rights the wrong committed
by King Saul, another Benjaminite, when he failed to kill Agag, King
of the Amalekites and ancestor of Haman.

Read each year as the central part of the Purim celebration, the
story of Esther has become sanitised – used as an excuse for chil-

dren to put on fancy dress and make noise and for adults to get drunk. But Esther is darker than this. At the end of the story, given the right to defend themselves, the Jews of Persia kill seventy-five thousand of their enemies (9:16). The story of Esther turns the normal order on its head: the disempowered minority becomes empowered, retaliating against those who once plotted against them; it is a fantasy of revenge. It is also in Bakhtinian terms an example of the literary carnivalesque. [5]

The use of peripety, the sudden reversal of fortune, as the book's main plot device is sometimes suggested as evidence for God's hand working in the background in the Book of Esther. Famously, the name of God – indeed any mention of God at all – is entirely lacking in Esther. Esther is one version, therefore, of the quintessential diaspora story – not a story of pious devotion to God who saves the faithful, but rather a story of wit and determination, of an assimilationist strategy that enables a subjugated people to save the day.

DANIEL

The two-part Book of Daniel is the only example of an apocalypse in the Hebrew Bible. Daniel 1–6 recounts court tales, while Daniel 7–12 describes apocalyptic visions. Traditionally the book is ascribed to Daniel himself, a Jew exiled to Babylon after the destruction of the Temple in 587/586 BCE. While the book's courtly legends may well have been oral traditions circulating for some time, the apocalyptic visions can be dated more accurately, as they contain historical allusions that make clear a knowledge of the Maccabean period. Specifically, these visions show knowledge of certain events, and were likely written after the events they describe in order to make these visions appear as accurate predictions. Where the visions veer off from established history, however, is at the end of the Maccabean revolt, allowing a fairly precise dating to 164 BCE.

---

5   The term, coined by the literary theorist Mikhail Bakhtin, refers to a story that upends the natural order – where the normal order and rules of everyday life are set aside. Elements both of playfulness and danger typify the carnivalesque, which takes its name from the traditional Catholic celebrations of Carnival before Lent.

The Book of Daniel is marked by an extensive use of Biblical Aramaic in Daniel 2–7. Curiously, this use of Biblical Aramaic spans both the court tales and the apocalyptic visions, perhaps in an attempt to unify the book's two sections. The court legends tell a story of pious devotion to God as a means of diasporic survival. In each of these stories, Daniel and/or his friends, Hannaniah, Mishael, and Azariah, are faced with existential threats – Daniel must interpret Nebuchadnezzar's dream or all the wise men will be killed; Daniel's friends must bow down to an idol or they will be thrown into a fiery furnace; Daniel must refrain from daily prayer or be thrown into a lion's den – and in each of these instances prayer, devotion to God, and remaining steadfastly Jewish (refusing, for example, to eat non-kosher food) save Daniel and his friends. In each situation, God works miracles for Daniel and his companions, saving them from vegan diets, conflagrations, and hungry lions, and sending miraculous dream interpretations to Daniel in his sleep. The Book of Daniel is the flip side of the story of Esther – a model for diasporic existence that relies on God's will.

The Book of Daniel has no regular public reading in Jewish practice. Additionally, though Daniel's own prayers have influenced Jewish liturgy, the book itself is little-used liturgically. Perhaps the best-known use of Daniel in Jewish prayer is Daniel 9:18–19, a supplication which forms part of the *ribbon ha'olamim* prayer in the *birkat hashaḥar* section of both daily and Shabbat morning prayers.

EZRA – NEHEMIAH

Although Ezra and Nehemiah are now printed as separate books, traditionally Jews have regarded them as a single work.[6] Current academic discussions question the unity of these works, particularly discussions looking at content rather than linguistic evaluations of the texts. This question of unity or separation also applies to the question of authorship. While some scholars have posited a single author for Ezra-Nehemiah and Chronicles, the subject is

---

6 The early Church father, Origen, began the practice of separating the books in the third century CE.

much contested and single authorship is now largely out of favor. Nevertheless, for the purposes of this introduction, Ezra-Nehemiah will be discussed under a single heading as per the traditional Jewish approach.

The dating of Ezra-Nehemiah to the fourth century BCE is widely accepted based on the historical references in the book itself. Textually, like Esther and Daniel, Ezra-Nehemiah has a complex history in both the Septuagint and Vulgate. 1 Esdras in the Septuagint (3 Esdras in the Vulgate), for example, is a translation of parts of 2 Chronicles, Ezra, and Nehemiah, with significant additions.[7] Also like the Book of Daniel, Ezra-Nehemiah contains significant portions written in Biblical Aramaic.

Together, Ezra-Nehemiah tells the story of the return of the exiles from Babylon and the rebuilding of the Temple in Jerusalem. Ezra begins at exactly the point at which 2 Chronicles ends, to the extent that Ezra 1:1–3a is identical to 2 Chronicles 36:22–23. The basic outline of Ezra is as follows: Cyrus decrees that the Jews are allowed to return to Jerusalem to rebuild the Temple. A list of the returning exiles is given, followed by a detailed history of Zerubbabel's attempts to reconstruct the Temple and restore Temple practices, including some conflicts along the way. In Ezra 7, Ezra himself finally joins the returnees, and much of the rest of the book is his memoir. The end of the book, Ezra 10, addresses the situation of intermarried returnees, along with a list of their names. The Book of Nehemiah describes the rebuilding of the city walls of Jerusalem, the reinstitution of festival observance and public reading of the Torah, and various legislative acts instigated by Nehemiah. Nehemiah 13 also discusses intermarriage.

The books of Ezra and Nehemiah do not have any significant liturgical usage in modern Jewish practice, but Ezra himself, in

---

7 Esdras is the Greek transliteration of the name Ezra. 1 Esdras, as it is named in the Septuagint (or 3 Esdras as the same work is named in the Vulgate), is a reworking of the biblical Book of Ezra that includes some material from 2 Chronicles and Nehemiah in addition to a large percentage of material from the biblical Book of Ezra. The versification is different and some reordering of material from the biblical book to the Septuagint occurs.

particular, served as a significant role model for the rabbis. The emphasis on public reading and interpreting the Torah, alongside the legislative acts in both books, became central to rabbinic thinking. In the rabbinic imagination, Ezra was transformed into a second Moses. Additionally, the debate begun in Ezra-Nehemiah around endogamy continues to be a key issue for Jewish communities up to the present day.

1 AND 2 CHRONICLES

The division of the Book of Chronicles dates back to the Septuagint, but has no basis in Jewish tradition and little basis in either a content or linguistic analysis of the books. Chronicles, therefore, will be treated here as a single work. The Hebrew title, *divrei hayamim*, literally means "the matters of the days," but is best rendered as "annals." Nevertheless, Chronicles should not be confused with the various annals referred to in the Book of Kings, as Chronicles postdates Kings. Indeed, the general consensus is that Chronicles dates to the mid-fourth century BCE, although dates between 400–250 BCE are discussed. Traditionally ascribed to Ezra, the general position is that Chronicles is the work of a single author, known as "The Chronicler," or perhaps is the work of a single school.

In Greek, the title of the work is Paraleipomenon, meaning "things left over," or "off to one side," indicating a particular view of the content of the book. Chronicles is, essentially, a repetition of a story already told in the Hebrew Bible – the history of the world from Adam to Cyrus's edict returning the exiles from Babylon. The first nine chapters are largely genealogies, with the narrative proper only beginning in 1 Chronicles 10. From there forward the story generally follows the books of Samuel and Kings. Yet differences, on occasion significant, occur between the texts of Samuel-Kings and Chronicles. For example, in Chronicles, the reign of Saul takes up only one chapter, 1 Chronicles 10, and the story of David seducing Bathsheba is completely absent. From 2 Chronicles 10 onwards, a variety of war reports appear that are not found in Kings. Numerous other both minor and more major differences abound, but, equally, some sections of Chronicles repeat, almost word-for-word, sections of Samuel and Kings.

Following from 1 Chronicles 10, the rest of Chronicles is broadly divided as follows:

- 1 Chronicles 11–29: David's reign
- 2 Chronicles 1–9: Solomon's reign
- 2 Chronicles 10:1–36:16: The reigns of Rehoboam through to Zedekiah
- 2 Chronicles 36:17–23: The destruction of the Temple and the walls of Jerusalem, exile, and Cyrus's decree

The real debate is whether, as the Septuagint title seems to imply, the Chronicler had access to versions of Samuel-Kings, either written or oral, which differ significantly from the Masoretic Text that he was working with as he filled out the story in Chronicles, or if he is creating a sort of commentary within the text itself – which would be known in modern interpretative theory as inner-biblical criticism – on Samuel-Kings, perhaps for political ends.

In Jewish communities Chronicles is, by and large, little known. The book has no liturgical use in the Jewish calendar and very few verses have made their way into either the daily or Shabbat liturgy.

CONCLUSION

As evidenced by the diversity of each of these eleven books, *Ketuvim* is not easy to summarize succinctly. Each of these works will have its own unique appeal – whether it be the spiritual comfort of the psalms, the theological challenge of Job, or the poetic beauty of Song of Songs. Perhaps because some of these works are relatively late (compared to Torah or parts of *Nevi'im*), and can therefore speak more immediately to us as modern readers, *Ketuvim* should have a more prominent place in the imagination of Jewish communities than it often does. One can read Lamentations and realise that the horrors it describes are as familiar (and horrific) to us today as they were to its readers and listeners two millennia ago. The wisdom of Ecclesiastes and Proverbs continues to address the same existential crises today as it did in antiquity. The return of the exiles as described in Ezra and Nehemiah may bring to mind our own return to the land of Israel in the twentieth century, as Esther and Daniel remind us of our own stories of exile and diaspora. And the books of Chronicles are perhaps among the earliest examples of political spin.

Individually these works are masterpieces in their own rights. Collectively they make up not only the most diverse of the three major sections of the Hebrew Bible, but also an infinitely fascinating and, at times, startlingly modern work.